Encyclopedic Deskbook of Teaching Ideas and Classroom Activities

by HAROLD I. COTLER

Here is the time-tested answer to the problem plaguing virtually *all* elementary teachers— where to find useful, relevant and practical activities for the class.

No longer need you spend those long hours searching through countless sources to find ideas and projects. Now, compiled in one complete A-to-Z volume, is a goldmine of ideas that will enable you to answer such questions as:

- **Where can I find, in one place, resources for units and daily lesson plans?**
- **How can I acquire *unique* ways to motivate my students?**
- **How can I develop meaningful activities to individualize my methods of instruction?**

This desk guide is an easy-to-use and modern sourcebook that contains the answers to these and many other questions. The format is that of an encyclopedia—an alphabetically organized tool to help meet your individual needs *and* those of the students.

SAVES TIME AND WORK!

If you have a problem with motivation, for example, simply look up the entry "Motivation." Numerous cross-references are provided to help you quickly solve a broad range of educational problems. And, each entry in the Deskbook can be easily adapted to your own particular background and style of teaching.

You will discover how to effectively plan and organize your methods of instruction. It contains detailed procedures to plan field trips, successful parent-teacher conferences and top-notch language arts instruction.

What's more, this educational master plan includes practical writing ideas, resources, interest centers, projects, materials for activity cards and assorted methods of instruction. Different, often ingenious, approaches to traditional subjects are presented—in a manner that virtually guarantees increased classroom discipline!

Here's a small example of the helpful hints you'll find in this valuable book:

- Poetry—here are more than *twenty* variations and forms for teaching your students to express themselves with verse . . .
- Newspaper — more than *ninety* activities for using the daily paper as an educational tool . . .
- Food — "The shortest path to a student's brain is through his stomach." Here are highly-effective uses of food in class . . .
- Sports — fascinating integration of sports concepts with the academic subjects — a learning experience for student *and* teacher . . .

plus much, much more!

Use this book and you will uncover the necessary information to develop motivational materials and activities for students. Most important of all—the theme of this guide is based on an integrative approach to the learning process, thus insuring that your pupils discover the true relationships between subject matter *and* real life.

Encyclopedic Deskbook
of Teaching Ideas
and Classroom Activities

Harold I. Cotler

Parker Publishing Company, Inc.
West Nyack, New York

Library of Congress Cataloging in Publication Data

Cotler, Harold I
  Encyclopedic deskbook of teaching ideas and classroom
activities.

  Includes index.
  1. Education, Elementary--Curricula--Handbooks,
manuals, etc. 2. Creative activities and seat work--
Handbooks, manuals, etc. I. Title.
LB1570.C84   372.1'3   76-49939
ISBN 0-13-275396-0

DEDICATION

This book is dedicated to the memory of my father,
Abe H. Cotler,
for his inspiration and support in my efforts,
and to my sister,
Julia A. Cotler,
for her artistic endeavors and never-ending encouragement.
It is also dedicated to my students—
past, present, and future—
without whom none of this would be possible.

A Word from the Author on the Unique, Practical Value This Book Offers . . . .

A problem that faces all elementary teachers is: Where can I find useful, relevant, and practical activities for my class? The *Encyclopedic Deskbook of Teaching Ideas and Classroom Activities* fills that need. Teachers do not want to spend endless hours searching through countless sources to find ideas and projects, and you will discover that this deskbook is a gold mine of ideas that will enable you to answer such questions as . . .

- Where can I find, in one place, sources and resources for units and daily lesson plans?
- How can I acquire *unique* ways to motivate my students?
- How can I develop meaningful activities to individualize my methods of instruction?
- How can I become the teacher I want to be?

The answers to these and many other questions will be found in this book.

The *Encyclopedic Deskbook of Teaching Ideas and Classroom Activities* is an easy-to-use and modern sourcebook for elementary school teachers. The format is that of an encyclopedia or deskbook—an alphabetically organized resource to help meet the needs of teachers and, in turn, help you to meet the needs of the students.

If you have a problem with motivation, for example, simply look up the entry "Motivation." Many cross-references are also provided to help you quickly solve a broad range of educational problems. Each entry in the Deskbook can be easily adapted to your own particular background and style of teaching. Many open-ended activities are included, and the ideas and materials presented are flexible and "alive." All of these ideas and activities have been used successfully in the classroom. As a teacher in the public schools, I wanted to fill a gap in elementary education—to provide an alternative book. This book provides the teacher with many alternatives in education.

Included in *Encyclopedic Deskbook of Teaching Ideas and Classroom Activities* are guidelines that describe practical, effective writing ideas, resources, interest centers, projects, materials for activity cards, and assorted methods of instruction. Different, often ingenious, approaches to traditional subjects are presented.

The basic theme is based on an integrative approach to the learning process, since the elementary teacher is a teacher of *all* subjects. During a social studies lesson, for example, an elementary teacher may also be teaching science, art, language arts, reading, career education, and mathematics. In this interrelated approach, the students learn the relationships between the subject matter and real life.

This alternative book provides you with the necessary information to develop high motivational materials and activities for the students. The use of student-made instructional materials is also presented.

When you need an activity to fill a period before dismissal . . . when you want to supplement materials presented in the textbook . . . when you need a special idea for social studies . . . turn to the *Encyclopedic Deskbook of Teaching Ideas and Classroom Activities.*

Here are some practical ideas that appear in the book:

Have you tried allowing your students to become A TEACHER FOR A LESSON? Teach an individual student a given lesson. The child will then present the lesson to the entire class. You will become a student during the lesson. The child will appreciate your role, and you may also acquire a fresh perspective by being a student for a period of time.

Have you tried creating a CITY OF YOUR OWN? You can create a city within your own classroom. This can be done in conjuction with series of lessons about local government. Many of the functions of cities can be performed in your classroom. The students will learn much about themselves and about government during the process.

Have the students in your class been part of a REWARD SYSTEM? Students are rewarded for completion of assignments and projects. They are "paid," using a form of currency which may be redeemed for various projects, privileges, and prizes. This can be used to increase the student motivation.

The resource materials and supplemental activities of the *Encyclopedic Deskbook of Teaching Ideas and Classroom Activities* will also encourage discussion and self-expression. It will help to encourage positive attitudes in the students by making the learning environment pleasant for both the teacher and the students.

The Encyclopedic Deskbook will help you realize your potential as an educator. It will make your classroom come alive with the sound of learning, and both students and teachers will rediscover the fun and joy of learning together.

Harold Irwin Cotler

The author wishes to gratefully acknowledge:

The faculty of the Dr. John H. Winslow School of Vineland, N.J., for their friendship and guidance in completing this project.

Julia A. Cotler for the illustrations and interest centers that appear in the book.

Mr. Charles J. Jansky, professional photographer, for his assistance in the preparation of photographic material.

Encyclopedic Deskbook
of Teaching Ideas
and Classroom Activities

— the first letter of the alphabet; the grade that means outstanding achievement; and the beginning of this book.

ACHIEVEMENT. Perhaps the basic goal of all education is achievement. If the students do not achieve during the process of education, their educational needs have not been met. All people need to feel a certain amount of achievement in their lives.

Nothing succeeds like success. When students have had success in school, they will continue to find success.

Try these suggestions for improving student achievement:

1. Allow the students to be an integral part of the planning process because they can contribute fresh ideas to the curriculum.

2. Establish individual conferences with the students to determine and communicate their achievement. This will also help you to know your students on a more personal level.

3. Have the students help other students. This is an aspect of education that we often forget. One-to-one instruction can work effectively. Try it.

4. Set up a series of learning contracts for the various subjects. (See CONTRACTS.)

5. Individualize your method of instruction. Try to reduce your total group instruction procedures. (See INDIVIDUALIZATION.)

ACHIEVEMENT MOTIVATION. Achievement motivation involves the teaching of students to think and act like high achievers. Motivation can be taught to students just as arithmetic, language, and art are taught.

Here are some suggested activities and ideas that will help to increase student achievement and motivation.

1. Have each student set a daily, weekly, and long-term goal. Have each one keep a record of his progress in achieving the goal.
2. Read the students stories and books that have an achievement theme. Many biographies and autobiographies fall into this category.
3. Hold discussions about successes and failures.
4. Plan a newspaper story for each student. The title of the imaginary article is "Outstanding Citizen Award." The student writes why he has received the award.
5. Use the concept of feedback to determine success.
6. Have the students make a list of "Things I Can Do."
7. Have the students make a list of "Things I Can't Do."
8. Have the students analyze their goals to determine which goals are unrealistic and which goals can be achieved.
9. Have the students write a news article about themselves.
10. Discuss the reasons why sports teams win or lose.
11. Have the students select several cartoon characters and determine which ones are successful.

ACHIEVEMENT TESTS. Teachers need to teach students how to take tests. Achievement tests give the teacher the opportunity to teach test format and the thought processes involved in taking a test.

1. Use spelling tests to teach format. Give the students four meanings for a word and have them select the best answer.

2. Use a selection from an encyclopedia, textbook, or reading book and make up a set of questions. The questions

should involve simple recall, inference, vocabulary development, and finding the main idea.

3. Write a paragraph with many grammatical errors. Tell
the students that there is a mistake in each line. Have them correct the paragraph.

4. Following directions is a difficult task. Make up a sample answer sheet to accompany a test. Have the students fill in
their names, ages, etc. Make up an answer key for a science test
and have the students use it with the test.

5. Make up a multiple choice test based on a reading
selection. Make the possible choices "A," "B," "C," "D," and
"None of the above."

6. Ditto a friendly letter with mistakes in grammar, spelling, punctuation, and form. Have the students correct the letter
and explain the corrections.

7. Write several sentences with punctuation errors. Give
the students choices of punctuation marks with which to complete the sentences.

8. Locate several weather maps or economic graphs and
charts from the newspaper. Make up several worksheets asking
the students questions about the graphs.

9. Bring in a sample of different types of maps—
population, road, graphic relief, rainfall, product, and vegeta-
tion. Set these up at an interest center. Have the students write
questions about them.

10. Develop an in-depth teaching unit on resource and
reference material. Spend several lessons on each of the
following: thesaurus, atlas, encyclopedia, glossary, index, card
catalog, almanac, newspaper, and telephone directory.

11. Mathematical skills must also be developed. (See
MATHEMATICS.)

ACTION WORDS. Variety is the spice of life. Variation of the
voice can add life to your classroom. This activity can be done
by both the students and the teacher.

In how many different ways can you say the following words and phrases? Try it. . .

yes	perhaps	no	never
see	don't	sorry	who me
well	possible	scared	really
guess	oh	tomorrow	please

Good morning. Are you the piano tuner?
I can't believe I ate the whole thing.
Sorry about that.

Discover some different ways to say the words:

| kindness | bashful | proud | sad |
| amused | surprised | disappointed | amazed |

Make a game of this. Your students and you will enjoy it.

ACTIVITY DAY.   An activity day is a learning experience for all involved. The activity day involves a series of physical education competitions between various grade levels.

Depending upon the grade level of your students, some of the activities may include three-legged races, one-hundred-yard dashes, sack races, baseball throw, football throw, baseball game, relay races, walkathons, tug-of-war, and volleyball games.

Blue ribbons can add excitement to the activity day.

The best time for this type of experience is in June. It helps to provide the needed motivation for positive behavior at this time of the year.

Organization of the activity day should be done with the help of the physical education specialists (if they are a part of your school faculty).

The students will long remember the competitions that took place during Activity Day. (See PHYSICAL EDUCATION.)

ADVERTISEMENTS. Advertisements offer the students a wide variety of learning experiences. Among them are these:

1. Have the students make an original product and "sell it" to the class.
2. Have the students look for various high pressure selling techniques such as "bandwagon," professional endorsements, and catchy songs. Report the results to the class.
3. Have the students verify the various advertisements to be sure that the ads are truthful and accurate.
4. Use newspapers to encourage competitive shopping.
5. Have the students develop activities that will test the product claims.
6. Sing several commercials from television and radio. Make up your own jingles.
7. Determine the cost of an advertisement on the radio, on television, and in the newspaper. Compare them.
8. Write an advertisement that could have appeared one hundred years ago.
9. Write an advertisement that might appear a hundred years from now.
10. Write an advertisement that advertises YOU. (See NEWSPAPERS.)

AFFECTIVE EDUCATION. Affective education involves the teaching of values and attitudes to students. Its counterpoint is known as cognitive education.

Affective education is relatively new, but in recent years it has come into its own. Affective curricula are being developed throughout the country.

Some activities for developing positive attitudes and values are:

1. Hold open and frank discussions of values and feelings. Do not attempt to criticize the values or comments. Accept them and discuss them.

2. Have the students make a list of the values they desire.
3. Use projective techniques such as:

I wish my teacher would . . . .
What I really want from life is . . . .

(See PROJECTIVE TECHNIQUES.)

4. Keep a diary.
5. Write a story called "The Real Me."
6. Draw a self-portrait of the *inside you.*
7. Have several role-playing sessions. This activity will help students to openly discuss values and problems.
8. Establish a problem. Have the students develop several alternative solutions to the problem.
9. Have a "close your eyes and think" session.
10. Hold a rap session known as a Magic Circle. (See MAGIC CIRCLE.)

AIDES (INSTRUCTIONAL). Instructional aides can help to improve the instruction in your classroom.

Some guidelines for instructional aides are as follows:

1. Aides should be treated on a professional level.
2. Aides should be given specific tasks or assignments.
3. Some tasks for aides are:
   a. Duplicate materials and tests.
   b. Set up learning centers.
   c. Work with small groups and individual problems to reinforce learning.
   d. Do clerical jobs, such as taking attendance, etc.
   e. Supervise students during physical education.
   f. Support the teacher and the teacher's methods.
   g. Assist the teacher with other tasks.
4. Aides should be given limitations for their work. They are not to be teachers, but aides to teachers.

AIDS (AUDIO-VISUAL). Some effective instructional activities that involve manipulatives follow:

1. Use silent counters in mathematics. Make them from sheets of plastic or use poker chips.

2. Take store signs and advertisements and make them into instructional charts and displays. Cover with clear Con-Tact paper.

3. Use clear acetate sheets to make transparencies. These sheets may be obtained from audio-visual dealers. Another source for acetate sheets is hospital X-ray laboratories. They will frequently give away used X-ray film which can be used with an overhead projector.

4. Inexpensive audio-visual aids may be made from unwoven cloth, lumber scraps, linoleum blocks, ceramic tiles, playing cards, and cardboard boxes.

5. Have the students bring in old games and puzzles. Repair and change these to develop new games and aids.

6. Use educational catalogs to observe new audio-visual aids. You can frequently make the same instructional tool at little or no cost.

ANIMALS. The study of animals can be effective at all grade levels. It is generally part of the science curriculum, but it can be adapted to all subjects in the curriculum.

The study of animals can be integrated into the following areas of instruction:

Science:
— Describe the animal. Tell what kind of animal it is (mammal, reptile, etc.).
— Compare the animal of your choice to another animal.
— Make a diagram of the animal in its habitat.
— Make a scale drawing of the animal.

Language Arts:
— Make a written and an oral report.
— Become an animal for a day. Tell your story.
— Make up words using the letters in the animal's name. (Tiger = Tony, idea, great, eat, red.)

— Tape record the oral report.

— What would happen if there were no tigers, etc.?

Social Studies:

— Locate the origin of the animals on a map.

— Trace the history of the animal on a chart.

— What kind of family does the animal have?

Art:

— Draw the animal with paint, tempera, crayons, or chalk.

— Draw the animal in the past and in the future.

— Make a stuffed animal with cloth.

— Make some transparencies.

— Make a papier mache animal.

Mathematics:

— Write several mathematics problems dealing with the animal of your choice.

— Make a chart comparing the speed, size, or location of the animal.

Career Education:

— Find out the occupations dealing with animals, such as marine biologist, veterinarian, and zoologist.

— Have a horse trainer or other individual involved with animals visit your class.

This is a sample of activities dealing with animals. You can add to the list.

ANTONYMS. Antonyms are words that are opposite in meaning to other words. They provide the opportunity to enrich a child's vocabulary.

1. Make a list of all the "anti-" words you can find. Match them with their meanings. Examples:

antacid	antarctic	antecede
antagonism	ante bellum	antedate

antemeridian	antibody	antipathy
ante mortem	anticline	antiseptic
antiaircraft	antifreeze	antislavery

2. When the students have new vocabulary words, have them write both synonyms and antonyms for them.

3. Make an interest center entitled "Antonym Andy" or "Antonym Annie." Have the students add words to the centers. Make a list of the new words presented during a month.

4. Make up a game in which the students are divided into two teams. One team calls out a word. The second team must provide an antonym within 15 seconds or lose a point. The game may be called "Antonym Antics." (See HOMONYMS AND SYNONYMS.)

ART PROJECTS. Elementary teachers use the art approach to enrich the curriculum. One problem with art projects is that materials are not always available for the project when you need them.

In order to avoid this problem, a list of materials is enclosed here. If you are aware of the materials, they will be available as needed. This list is by no means totally comprehensive. You can add to it as you find different or alternative materials.

Storage for the materials can be a problem. Assorted boxes or containers can help. Some of the materials may be stored at home. Students can help bring in materials for the projects. Use the list. Let your students enjoy art.

Here's a list of materials you can collect for art projects:

acetate	books	cereal boxes
aluminum foil	boxes	charcoal
artificial fruit	brace	clay
artificial plants	buttons	cloth
bags	camera	clothespins
balloons	cardboard	coins
beads	cards	compasses
bits (drill)	carpet remnants	construction paper

cornstarch
cotton
cups
darning needles
doweling
drill
easels
egg cartons
emery cloth
envelopes
feathers
film
finger paint
flour
glue
hammer
hangers
index cards
India ink
ink pad
jars
keys
lattice
leather
lint (from dryer)
loom
loops
macaroni
magazines
markers
meat trays
milk cartons
nails
needles

newspaper
nylon stockings
oak tag
orange juice
  cartons
paint
paintbrushes
paper clips
paper fasteners
paper plates
paper scraps
paper towels
papier mache
paste
pastels
pencils
picture frames
pipe cleaners
plaster of Paris
plastic containers
plasticene
plastic wrap
rags
realia
ribbon
rice
rulers
safety pins
sand
sandpaper
saws
scissors
screws
seeds

shells
shoeboxes
sponges
spools
stamps
stapler
staples
sticks
stones
straight pins
straws
string
styrofoam
tacks
tape
tempera
tile samples
tin cans
tin snips
tissue paper
tongue depressors
toys
TV Guides
watercolors
wax
waxed paper
window shades
wire
wood
wool
wrapping paper
yardstick
yarn

AWARDS. Everyone needs to be told, "You have done a good job." Contests in school can tell all the students that they have done well. Contests can also be learning experiences as well as fun.

An example of a contest is "Make a Word." Using the letters in the words "INDEPENDENCE DAY," make as many words from them as you can. Examples: deep, depend, need.

Give an award to the winner of the contest. Other awards can be given for attendance, outstanding achievement, outstanding achievement in physical education, handwriting excellence, commendable work in the various subjects, and spelling bees.

A small ribbon or award button can recognize the outstanding individual. You can also send home a letter of congratulations. This official effort will bring many rewards in the form of positive attitudes and positive behavior. TRY IT!

— the second letter of the alphabet; the grade that means above average achievement; and beauty, which is a part of the learning environment.

BEHAVIOR.   Behavior problems frequently arise. How does the experienced teacher handle them?

1. Talk to each child individually. Ask him to give reasons for his behavior (if possible). Talk to him before or after class.

2. Set up an individual behavior modification contract with a child. Establish a mutual goal towards which he will work. The initial goal may be to have him stop calling out for a period of two days —or even one. Constant encouragement is needed. When the child achieves the initial goal, set up an additional one which he can achieve. (See ACHIEVEMENT MOTIVATION.)

3. Have the child write down his feelings after an incident in the classroom. You should also write down your feelings. Exchange the papers with the student. Discuss the problems with him. Treat the child with respect. Try to reach a mutual solution to the problem.

4. Use nonverbal communication to eliminate behavior problems before they start. These clues—looks, smiles, and touching—can serve as rewards for good behavior and reminders to the other students. A tap on the shoulder—a stern look—a genuine smile—a handshake—given at the appropriate time can help alleviate problems.

5. As another possible solution to problems, analyze the child's behavior in terms of your teaching. Consider the physical, social, and emotional aspects of a child.

BOOK FAIR. Book distributors will arrange a book fair for your school. This consists of a vast display of books which the students may purchase. Most of the books are paperbacks, and many cost less than a dollar.

Some book fairs are available in a trailer with built-in shelves for the books. The school receives a certain percentage from the sales.

A book fair can be combined with a student display of projects, and can be an excellent fund-raising activity. Consider it for your school.

BOOK REPORTS. Book reports do not have to be distasteful for both the teacher and the students. Here are some ways to make such reports non-toxic for the students:

1. Have the students write a book review for a newspaper. Use the style found in real newspapers as a guide.
2. Make a bulletin board, mural, or frieze to depict a part of the book that you enjoyed.
3. Make a hand puppet or a paper bag puppet of one of the characters in the story.
4. Write a letter to the author and/or publisher telling why you liked or didn't like the book. You may also make suggestions about the book.
5. Write an original poem or creative piece which was inspired by reading the story.
6. Become one of the characters in the story. Dress like that individual. Tell your part of the story.
7. Prepare a chalk talk for the class.
8. If you read a "how-to" book, bring in your creative effort.
9. Make a miniature scene or a diorama based upon the theme of the story.

10. Make a set of unusual illustrations that exhibit the highlights of the book.
11. Re-write the ending of the story.
12. Re-do the cover of the book in your own design.
13. Bind your own original book. Put it in the school library.
14. Make a report of the book and present it to another class.
15. Hold a round-table discussion of the book.

The important thing to remember about book reports is that they do not have to be written. Use other media to reach the goal of book reports. You can use the strengths of the students.

BOOKS. Innovative techniques for using books can motivate your students to read more books.

1. Select a short book. Have the students re-write it and change all the nouns and/or verbs in the book. Compare the students' story to the original version.

2. Have the students write an original book and submit it to a children's publisher. The experience will prove very worthwhile. Many unexpected learnings will also take place.

3. Write original books and place them in the class library or the school library. Have the students make up author, title, and subject cards for the library's card catalog.

4. Make up a "What Am I" game for use with books. Put the questions on index cards. Make up an answer key which the students may use.

"I cover the book."	book cover
"I am found on the cover."	title
"I wrote the book."	author
"I am a date."	copyright date
"I am the place where the book was printed."	city of publishing company
"I tell what's in the book."	table of contents
"I am on every page in numerical order."	page numbers

"I am the largest part of a book."   body or content
"I am the last part of the text."   index
"I am the book's backbone."   spine

5. Have the students design a book cover to replace those covers that have worn out. Make a bulletin board with book covers. Make a game of book covers by covering all the words on a cover, leaving just the pictures or illustrations. Have the students guess the book's identity.

BRAINSTORMING. Brainstorming is a process that encourages students to participate in suggesting ideas related to a specific theme or problem.

For example, a topic of discussion may be the problems of the playground. A round-table discussion is held. Many possible solutions to the problem are given by the students and the teacher. The effects of each solution can be discussed in depth.

Brainstorming can also be applied to suggesting ideas for creative writing, proposing ideas for various units of instruction, and solving various problems.

The important idea behind the brainstorming sessions is to accept all of the student responses. If you respond negatively to their comments, the session will not be very productive. Brainstorming is also helpful because it involves the students in the process of education.

BULLETIN BOARDS. Bulletin boards should be informative as well as attractive. There should be a purpose behind them. They are not just objects with which to fill space.

Allow the students to work on the bulletin boards. With your assistance the students (at the elementary level) can make them. They will pay more attention to bulletin boards that they made themselves. Primary students can assist by making projects and art efforts to put on the board.

A suggestion: Modify the bulletin boards each year and several times each month. It will help to make the room a real learning center.

Here are some suggestions for bulletin boards throughout the school year:

January:

Roman Mythology—Janus
We're #1
Ring My Chimes for the New Year
The Birth of a Nation (New Year)

February:

Leaders of America
February Is for Lovers! (Valentines)
Groundhog—Do Your Thing!!
We're Small but Mighty (short month)
Leap Year—JUMP!

March:

March Forth and Forward March
How to Grow a Boat (see Figure 1.)
Windy Month in a Windy Place
When Irish Eyes Are Laughing
Spring Has Sprung

April:

The Rain in Spain Also Falls Here
Patriots' Day—Hooray!!
Plant That Tree (Arbor Day)
Spring—Where Are You?

May:

Mother *May* I? (language)
J. F. K. in May (birthday)
Laws—Who Needs Them? WE DO.
May Day!! May Day!!

June:

It's June in January (in South America)
Watch Out, Summer—You're Here Now

FIGURE 1: **How to Grow a Boat**

D-Day
Summer Countdown—10 9 8 7 6 5 4 3 2 1

July:

Julius Caesar Did It
Sun and Fun for All and One
On the Fourth—Remember
Let's Declare This. . .

August:

Augustus Caesar Did It
School's Almost Here
Farm Time Is Just Now
Columbus Landed Early

September:

September Is Here and So Are You
Labor Day—WORK, WORK, WORK
World Series Time—Strike Three
Sign the Constitution (signed in 1787)

October:

Pumpkin, Pumpkin, Shining Bright
Octagon, October, Ocho (8)—HOW?
Harvest Time During Indian Summer
UNITED NATIONS—Do Your Thing!!

November:

Football, U.S.A.
Vote—It's Your Right and Duty
Be Thankful for. . .
Getting Chilly—Button Up

December:

December, Decagon, Decimal—FIND OUT
It's Almost Over
Ice Hockey Time
Winter—Brrrrrrrrrrrrrrrrrrrrrrrr!

— the third letter of the alphabet; the grade that means average; and colorful, which classrooms should be.

CALENDAR ACTIVITIES.   The calendar offers a wide variety of learning experiences for students.

At the primary level, the calendar can be used to reinforce various number skills and counting procedures. It can be an integral part of the early morning activities, which include the weather, discussion of the days of the week, and other current events.

Each student can have an individual calendar on his desk. Calendars may also be used as an art project.

At the intermediate level, you can develop several mathematical problems relating to the calendar:

If the 3rd of January falls on a Wednesday, on what day will the 7th of June fall? (Figure it out yourself first.)

Have the students make several problems like this one. Put them on ditto masters and run them off for the class.

Allow the students to design a calendar of the future. Display these throughout the classroom.

Make a calendar with various mathematical facts equal to each day of the month.

Have the students draw a psychedelic calendar as an art project.

Your students can write stories or poems about the topic "Our days are numbered."

If your students study different bases in mathematics, have them make a base 5 calendar.

Keep a calendar of the number of days left in the school year. Make this a prominent display.

Have the students do a research project by using the entry "calendar" in the encyclopedia.

Develop your own activities dealing with the months and days of the year.

CAMERA. A camera is a *must* for every classroom from kindergarten through post graduate work. Some of the effective ways in which a camera can be used in a classroom are listed here:

—Take pictures on the first day of the school year. Make them into a "Begin the Year with a Smile" bulletin board.

—Take pictures of the children and select one as the "Student of the Week." This bulletin board or display area contains the picture of the student and any other items the child would like to display. He can also wear a "Student of the Week" button.

—When you have a special project or activity, the camera is available to record the event. Too often there are many scenes you would like to have recorded, but there was no camera available.

—The camera may also be used to permanently record your favorite bulletin boards.

—Teach your students to use the camera. They can use their knowledge of the camera to help them with reports and projects.

—Make a scrapbook with the pictures taken during the year. Let the students write captions for the pictures.

The 126- or 110-cartridge cameras are convenient for use in a classroom. Regardless of the type of camera, have one available and use it frequently.

CAREER EDUCATION.   Career education integrates the world of work into the elementary school curriculum. It is NOT a separate subject or a separate curriculum.

Some of the ways career education can become part of your classroom are:

1. Study various occupations such as mechanic, carpenter, worker in the health field, teacher, and space engineer. This may involve the language arts, social studies, and the sciences.

2. Measure the room to find how much rug is needed to cover the floor. Other measurement activities could involve the playground, halls, and walls. Relate this to the careers of painters, lumbermen, carpet layers, and architects.

3. Read some books about various occupations and famous people. Find out what special parts of the occupations the people enjoyed. How did each person become a doctor, lawyer, or truckdriver? Write about the occupations.

4. Have the students list the requirements for becoming an electrician, teacher, or politician. Allow them to select any occupation.

5. Make a bulletin board and display of various occupations. Write a story or poem about each.

6. Make a list of the jargon of different professions. Train engineers, for instance, have a specialized vocabulary. Prepare a speech using the jargon of some industry or profession.

7. Research the history of various occupations such as whaling and farming to determine the changes that have taken place over the years.

8. Invite various people from the community to visit your classroom. Don't forget to include the parents of your students. (See COMMUNITY RESOURCES.)

9. Develop a central directory of occupations. Each child can contribute to this card catalog or booklet. The directory can include the title of the occupation, its description, and the qualifications for the job. It can also list some of the people who practice the occupation.

You may add to this sampling. Career education puts the school day into the real world. School can become more meaningful if the students realize that it is a preparation for life.

CHARTS. Charts are appropriate for all levels of education and for all subjects in the curriculum.

To be effective, charts should be prepared using the following guidelines:

1. Charts should be colorful and attractive.
2. Permanent markers or colors should be used.
3. If it is possible, laminate the charts with a clear plastic or Con-Tact paper.
4. Charts should have a definite educational purpose.
5. Heavy tagboard or chart paper should be used.
6. The size of the chart should be appropriate for its use.
7. Letters and illustrations should be neat and clear.
8. Charts should assist the teacher or students in developing a concept.
9. Charts should be stored carefully so they may be used again.
10. Mailing tubes serve well in storing charts and similar materials.

Don't forget that your students may assist you in making charts. Use their artistic talents to enrich your classroom.

COMMUNITY RESOURCES. Effective elementary schools involve themselves with the entire community. Bringing the community into the school helps both the school and the people in the community.

Many people from the community are available to enhance the curriculum. Some resources appropriate at the elementary level are policemen, firemen, lawyers, doctors, forest rangers, county agricultural agents, naturalists, and professional athletes.

All of these and many others are willing to visit your classroom as a means of enrichment for a given unit. The students will greatly benefit from seeing people from the world of work.

Make the contacts well in advance. Be sure that the speaker is familiar with your goals and the level of instruction. Make the community a vital part of your elementary classroom.

COMPETITION. Competition is a part of the real world, yet some educators suggest that competition should be avoided in the schools. School is not an isolated social situation. It should reflect the world outside the classroom walls.

In order to make competition a positive force, each child should have an opportunity to suceed. For this reason, the activities and projects must be varied to meet individual needs and abilities.

Physical competition is a good area in which to develop teamwork and group cohesiveness. Activities may include races, free throws, football throws, walking, and assorted relays. Sportsmanship should be encouraged at all times.

Other devices to foster competition are spelling contests, art exhibitions, creative endeavors, make-a-word contests, speaking activities, and math games.

Students will learn the thrill of victory and also how to accept failure. Use the competition to help foster positive attitudes on the part of the students. (See AWARDS.)

COMPREHENSION. Comprehension is a basic goal of all instruction. Did my students learn what *I* wanted them to learn? Did the students learn what *they* wanted to learn? Did *any* learning take place during the course of the lessons?

Here are some ways to increase and improve student comprehension:

1. Have a student go to the front of the classroom and allow other students to question him on a specific unit of instruction. This should be done on a voluntary basis.

2. Allow the students to make up questions for a test. They must answer the questions themselves first.

3. Play a game such as "To Tell the Truth." Three students give answers to a question. Members of the class decide upon the correct choice.

4. Try to use oral questions instead of written tests to determine comprehension.

5. Have the students write a paragraph that gives the highlights of the article or story they read.

6. Use checklists, rating scales, and conferences as other devices to test comprehension. (See EVALUATION.)

7. Use role playing to enrich the evaluation process. Students will need to know the basics in order to play the appropriate roles.

8. Use bulletin boards, art projects, friezes, and dioramas for your own purposes in determining comprehension.

As most experienced teachers realize, it is not always necessary to use written devices in order to evaluate student comprehension.

CONCEPTS.   Concepts can be difficult to develop and difficult for the students to comprehend. Great care must be given to concept development.

In order to understand the idea of "concepts," here is an example of one:

A social studies concept is that of a *role*. Many experiences are necessary to develop this concept into the generalization that people in society serve many roles in their lives.

Some activities that can be used to develop the concept of *role* are:

1. Define the word by using the dictionary and also the experiences of the students.

2. List the roles that you play. These may include student, son or daughter, baseball player, patient, or sister.

3. Change the roles in your classroom. Become a student for a short period of time. Allow one of your students to teach a lesson.

4. Stage an incident in the classroom. Have the students write down the various roles that were played. Hold a discussion of the incident.

5. Discuss and portray the roles of the parents vs. the roles of the students. Have one child play both roles.

6. Have a student imagine and portray the role of a new student. Ask him to share his deep feelings and tell about the problems a new student faces in a new situation.

7. Play the role of a blind person. Have the students write their feelings.

8. List some of the roles you would like to play during your life.

9. Make a list of reasons why you like or dislike your roles as students and children.

Add to the list with your own ideas for your own classroom. (See ROLE PLAYING.)

Concepts may be developed at all levels of instruction. An example of a concept, *role*, has been given. But what exactly is a concept? A concept may be defined as a statement or series of statements that places ideas, events, or objects in a category. Concepts are not the memorization of individual facts.

Evaluate your teaching. Are you teaching concepts or facts? Decide.

CONFERENCES (PARENT AND TEACHER). Parent-teacher conferences help both the parents and the teachers to understand the child.

Three stages are needed for successful conferences: pre-planning, the actual conference, and the follow-up.

Pre-planning: Before a parent conference, whether it is for a specific problem or a regularly scheduled one, preparation is necessary.

A checklist or a series of statements on a worksheet will prepare you for the conference. The list may include specific strengths or weaknesses of the student, areas to be discussed during the conference, things the parent can do to help, questions you would like to have answered, and other relevant information.

If you don't do your homework, the conference will not be as successful as it could have been.

Schedule the conference with the parents' convenience in mind. Friday afternoon is not a good time for conferences. Know the rules of the school and your specific classroom guidelines. These may be a part of the conference.

The Conference Itself: The first thing to do in getting ready for conference is to remember not to be nervous!

1. Be friendly. Your positive approach is very important in establishing a good relationship.

2. Set a reasonable time limit for the conference. If you have conferences for all the students, the limit could be ten to fifteen minutes. If the conference is for only one child, the limits may be lifted.

3. Say something positive about the child. This is a vital part of the conference.

4. Be honest with parents, but do not be overly critical of the children.

5. Sit facing the parent. The chairs should be of equal heights. Don't sit behind your desk. It becomes a barrier to communication.

6. Do not talk all the time. Sometimes it is more profitable to listen to the parents.

7. Do not give the parents suggestions on how to raise their children.

8. If there is a specific problem, you may indicate how it was solved in another situation. Don't give specific names of students.

9. Avoid educational jargon. Tell what you want to say, but don't cloud the issue with jargon.

10. Avoid references to other members of the family or other teachers. Parents sometimes want to blame others for their problems. The conference must be held in a professional manner.

11. Leave the parent with the feeling that the conference was worth the effort.

The Follow-up: The follow-up is also an important part of the conference procedure.

1. Record your impressions of the conference.

2. List the items discussed and plans of action that will be taken by the parent, the child, and you.

3. If an additional conference is needed, plan it.

4. A teacher-child conference may also be helpful to relate courses of action for the child.

5. If a definite plan of action was established during the conference, put the plan into effect.

6. Keep a record of the conference. It may be placed in the cumulative folder. This record will help other teachers to develop a better understanding of the child.

Conferences are held for the benefit of all. Remember this the next time you have one.

CONTEXT.   Context clues are a basic part of teaching a child to read.

1. Place a sentence on the board and have the students analyze it for context clues. Example: "The famous baseball player traveled *incognito*. He wore dark glasses and a raincoat." Have the students tell which sentence gave them the most help.

2. Vary the format for context clues. Have the students complete a sentence with the last word: "The car salesman said, 'Let's make a ___.' " [keel—reel—deal—steel] After the students have become familiar with this format, have them make up context clues.

41

3. Bring in different meanings for a word and use it in context. An example is the word "expire." It may mean "to die," "to exhale," or "to terminate." Have the students choose the correct definition based on this sentence: "The motorist was given a ticket because his registration had expired."

4. Make up a series of context clues with a nonsense word. Have the students describe it to the best of their abilities.

    a. The *jangus* is alive.
    b. It lives in the jungles of Brazil.
    c. The wingspan of the jangus is seven feet. (First good clue.)
    d. The jangus produces a tricolored egg. (Good clue.)
    e. The diet of the jangus is flying insects.
    What is it? (Some kind of large bird, perhaps?)

CONTRACTS (LEARNING). Learning contracts are a series of activities and tasks that a student and teacher develop cooperatively. Guidelines include specific tasks that the child must complete, due dates, audio-visual aids, reading assignments, and lists of projects.

A sample learning contract is shown in Figure 2.

CONVERSATION. Everyone needs to talk, especially students. Proper encouragement will result in the full utilization of the art of conversation.

Here are some ways to involve your students in conversation:

1. Practice making imaginary telephone calls. This technique may also be used to develop proper telephone courtesy.
2. Films, booklets, and telephone training programs may be available through your local telephone company.
3. Have the students give a one-minute speech to sell a real or imaginary product. (See ADVERTISEMENTS.)

LEARNING CONTRACT

Due Date: _____

We, the undersigned, do hereby resolve to do the following projects about the unit New Jersey. At the completion of this contract, the reward of A will be received.

1. On a blank map of New Jersey, fill in the names of the counties, Trenton, the Atlantic Ocean, and the Delaware River.
2. Make a salt, flour, and water map of your county.
3. Use three reference books to find the names of three famous New Jersey inventors. Write a report about each.
4. Select a theme and decorate the front bulletin board.
5. Write an original story about one of the products of the state.
6. Select three math activity cards and solve the problems. Check your answers with the answer key.
7. Read chapters 1-4 in your text.

_____
(student's signature)

_____
(teacher's signature)

FIGURE 2: **Sample Learning Contract**

4. Have a "talkathon." Allow the students to talk to anyone for fifteen minutes. They may choose any topic.
5. Have a period of silence during the day. Discuss how the silence feels.
6. Use the tape recorder to record conversations and speeches.
7. Imagine that you are at a party. Hold a nonsense conversation with three people.
8. Make an estimate of the amount of time people talk during a day. Find out how much you talk.
9. Play the role of a telephone operator.
10. Listen to a radio broadcast. What types of conversations did you hear? Make your own radio broadcast.

CREATIVE WRITING. Creative writing is one area of the curriculum that can be fun for both the teacher and the students. It should not be a regimented subject. Creative writing should be a free expression of the student's ideas and style.

Creative writing should not be evaluated in the same manner as other subjects. Assignments should be read by the teacher and appropriate comments should be made.

1. Read a folk tale to the class. Have the students re-write it, but change the names to protect the innocent.

2. Since a picture is worth 1,000 words, have the students write 1,000 words about a picture. Divide 1,000 by the number of students in the class, and have each person write 35 or 40 words about the picture.

3. MY OPINION IS. . . . Have the students select a topic of their choice. Have them write their opinions in 100 words or less.

4. WHAT IF. . . . Write several statements on the board. Have the students select one and write about it.

> "What if . . . all the television sets in the world were
> broken?"
> . . . All the cars ran in reverse."
> . . . all the highways melted?"
> . . . push-buttons pushed back?

5. Place the title "The Case of the Missing _____" on a sheet of paper. List several possible completing words— "teacher," "rabbit," "taco," "gasoline"—and have the students select one and complete the assignment.

6. Make up an original dictionary. Have the entire class contribute to the book. Some possible original dictionaries are tools, dictionary of sports, and dictionary of modern expressions.

7. Have the students write a story about themselves. All the characters in the story must be the students themselves. The title of the story may be "Believe It or Else."

8. Have the students write a series of false statements or statements which are total exaggerations. Have them illustrate the assignment.

9. Have the students write about "The Day the Sun Refused to Shine." Relate this to the problems of pollution.

10. PEANUT PROSE. Give each child an unshelled peanut. Have the students describe the peanut, name it, and give it an imaginary personality. Have the students make it into a pet peanut. Have the students write the life history of their pet peanut. Do the same activity with a rock or other interesting object.

Other formats for creative writing assignments are:

11. If I were a _____. Have the students fill in the blanks with ideas.

12. If I had a _____.

13. My wishes are _____. Allow the students to make three magic wishes.

14. Write descriptions to pictures from a magazine.

15. Write stories about colors, sounds, or shapes.

> Red is _____.
> Barking is _____.
> Square is _____.

16. Rewrite a nursery rhyme.

17. Describe happy or sad things.

18. Write about "The Me Inside of Me."

19. Write some proverbs or slogans.

20. "Do your own thing." Allow the students to select their own style or format for creative expression.

CREATIVITY. Creativity lies in the mind of the beholder. "If I think I am creative, therefore I am."

Both the teacher and the students can increase each other's creativity. Schools should encourage creativity—to have each individual develop to his ability.

How to Be Creative As a Teacher:

1. Constantly seek new and innovative ways to teach your lessons. Don't be satisfied with the old ways.

2. Constantly reevaluate your performance with the goal of improvement in your mind.

3. If you are especially artistic or skilled in a musical way, use this skill to enhance your teaching.

4. Don't blame others for problems. Find your own solutions.

5. Use a variety of media in your teaching. The students will tire of the same thing every day. Vary your approaches to learning.

6. Continue to be enthusiastic about your teaching and toward your students.

7. Share ideas with other teachers and other professionals. You can always learn from others.

8. Learn from your students. Learning is a sharing process that can benefit both the teacher and the students.

9. BE YOURSELF. This is probably the most important part of teaching. Don't try to copy the teacher across the hall.

How to Let Your Students Be Creative:

Students also are creative—or can be (if teachers let them).

1. Allow the students to participate in planning units of study and classroom activities.

2. Don't require the same assignments of all students. Each student needs different assignments.

3. Allow the students a freedom of choice in the classroom.

4. Let the students share their feelings with you and let them contribute to the curriculum.

5. Let the students visit the library or instructional media center with a great deal of frequency.

6. Encourage the students to participate in the creation of bulletin boards and projects.

7. Allow the students to move around the room as needed.

8. Let the students be themselves.

CRITICAL READING. Critical reading skills are extremely difficult for students to grasp.

Some critical reading and study skills at the elementary level follow:

1. Use of sources and resources such as a dictionary, encyclopedia, thesaurus, and other reference materials.

2. Use of parts of books, such as the table of contents, glossary, and index.

3. Ability to locate information from picture clues, captions, and labels.

4. Recognition of the main ideas of paragraphs.

5. Understanding the different purposes of reading—for enjoyment, for information, to answer questions, and to check details.

6. Recognition of the style of a writer and the plot of a story.

7. Understanding the different types of literature.

8. Ability to make logical inferences and draw conclusions from materials read.

9. Understanding the use of charts, graphs, and illustrations.

Each of these skills must be handled at your level of instruction. You can provide these activities by developing materials that will challenge the students and allow them to meet success in each area. (See READING.)

CURIOSITY. Curiosity may have killed the cat, but it can enliven your classroom. Children are naturally curious. They want to know the unknown. As an elementary teacher, you must not dampen your students' curiosity.

During the first snowfall of the year your students are extremely curious and interested. You have a choice—close the shades, or use the teaching situation to its fullest. Which choice is yours? You can turn off the students or you can use their enthusiasm to make learning fun.

An important event is happening—a special space event, a world crisis, or the World Series. Will you turn off their interest by saying, "We can't talk about that now," or. . . ?

Use the student concern to teach them. In the final analysis, the choice is yours.

CURRICULUM. The curriculum consists of all the planned and unplanned activities and experiences the students have. In addition to the physical facilities, it consists of the basic subjects—reading, writing, and arithmetic, as well as social studies, science, health, music, and physical education.

The more informal aspect of the curriculum involves the socialization process, free time, lunch, and extracurriculars.

A teacher's influence is most felt in the formal area. Your influence to improve the curriculum should be exerted.

Your attitudes and comments will have a profound effect upon the students. It is often this intangible area that means the most to them.

— the fourth letter of the alphabet; a grade that means passing work; and for democracy— the basis of America.

DECISION-MAKING PROCESS. Students frequently feel that adults make all the decisions, and that they are left out of the decision-making process.

You can change this misconception by the following:

1. Allow the students to select a choice among several assignments at an interest center.

2. Set up a system of checks and balances in your class. If some students are having problems, have other students make suggestions for improving the situation.

3. Discuss the role of people in government. (See DEMOCRACY.)

4. Establish a suggestion box in the room. Discuss the suggestions during a class meeting.

5. Allow the students to participate in the determination of sequences of units, experiences, and activities for the class. Their ideas will complement yours.

DEMOCRACY. How can we teach children about a democratic form of government? This problem arises frequently in the elementary classroom. The concept of democracy is an abstract one, but the teacher can bring it to a more concrete level.

A 100% pure democracy in a classroom would not work. The students would outvote the teacher on many issues. But the students and the teacher can work together to insure the life of the democratic process.

The students can vote on many matters. They can have class presidents. They can decide upon assorted jobs for the classroom.

In the social studies area, the students can re-enact some of the historical events that have led up to today. They can establish a mini-government within the class. Field trips to local or state government buildings will also enhance classroom learnings.

DEVELOPMENTAL TASKS. Developmental tasks are various levels students must face during the process of growth and maturation.

The areas for development are:

1. Physical: The child must adapt to his growth pattern and accept himself. The role of the teacher in this capacity is to also accept the child. As part of your instruction, deal with individual differences. Explain the differences in growth rates. This will help the child to adjust to problems that may arise.

2. Social: In this area of development, the child learns to relate to his peers, to develop his self-concept, and to develop his role in life as a male or a female.

The teacher, by example and instruction, can foster good human relationships between the class and himself. He can also provide activities like the following:

a. Write a book about yourself. Illustrate it.
b. Read books that illustrate the different roles of males and females in society.
c. Write stories with such titles as "The Real Me" or "My Inside Me and My Outside Me."
d. Have the students keep diaries in which to write their feelings about school and home.

3. Emotional and Mental: In this area, the student develops a good set of values and attitudes. He also is developing good mental health ideas.

The teacher can do much in this area by rewarding positive behavior. The teacher's attitude also serves as an example for the student. The students will frequently imitate the behavior of the teacher and will adopt or adapt his ideas.

DIAGNOSIS. The diagnosis of student problems is a basic activity that will help to foster success in the school situation.

Your task is to find out if the child is in some type of trouble or has a certain type of problem.

Some guides for observation are:

1. Does the child have difficulty seeing the board?
2. Does he have a limited attention span or bore easily?
3. Does he misread words or substitute words frequently?
4. Does he have difficulty in hearing your directions?
5. Is he constantly in"trouble"?
6. Does he have difficulty in writing or in completing assignments on time?

You can add to this brief list. The source of the problem may be physical, social, or emotional (or a combination of these).

If you feel that a child is having a serious learning difficulty, where do you turn?

You can turn to the cumulative records, previous teachers of the child, parent conferences, and conferences with the child. Ask your principal for help. See the nurse, too.

If appropriate in your school situation, involve the child study team or the learning disabilities specialist. (See READING.)

DICTIONARY GAMES. The dictionary in the elementary classroom can be both educational and fun. Here are some games that can be played in your classroom:

1. Dictionary Race: (Grade 3 and up: Organize the class into several even groups arranged in rows or in a straight line. Place several words on the board for the students to define. At the given moment, pass the dictionaries back to the students. The first student in line will define the first word. He will give the dictionary to student 2, and so on. The first student group to finish is the winner. Be sure that each member of the group knows the given word. The levels of difficulty and the time involved will vary with the grade level.

2. Olé!—Foreign Dictionary Game: If you can obtain several foreign dictionaries, develop a worksheet that gives the student a chance to use the dictionary. You may also make signs in a foreign language and place them around the room. Set up an interest center based on the language. If you are able to, teach the students a few basic words of Spanish, French, or some other language. Adapt the Dictionary Race to Olé.

3. The Yes or No Game: In this activity, the students write questions that can be answered with only a *yes* or a *no*. The questions are based on words in the dictionary.

Example: Can a spinet spin a web?   (NO.)

The questions may be duplicated or placed on the board. This activity may be done with the whole group or with part of the class. The Yes or No Game can be used to develop student vocabularies. The children will enjoy this game because it will challenge them.

4. Jolly Good Show: Have the students find in the dictionary several words that have British spellings. Place both spellings on the board and have the students guess which is the American spelling and which is the British one. Use the dictionary to double-check the answers. This can also be adapted to an interest center.

5. fō nĕt´ ĭk: Write directions for a worksheet or a test phonetically, using the guide in your dictionary. Have the students write the answers to the questions phonetically. This game will reinforce your skill lessons in reading and also in language arts.

6. Abbreviated: Abbreviations frequently create problems. Use the want ads and the classified section of the newspaper to develop abbreviations.

In the car ads you might find something like this: Used car—excel. cond., hdtp., auto., 8 cyl., ps, air, ww, am/fm, 350 eng., 4 dr. Chp.

This may be translated to: Used car—excellent condition, hardtop, automatic, 8 cylinders, power steering, air conditioner, white walls, AM and FM radio, 350 cubic inch engine, four doors. Cheap.

A similar project may be done with ads for apartments or houses. The students may also write ads using other abbreviations.

7. No Nonsense Here: Make up a list of nonsense words and place them on the board or on a ditto. Have the students write imaginary definitions for these words. Use them in sentences.

8. DICTIONARY: Write the letters d-i-c-t-i-o-n-a-r-y on the blackboard. Have the students make up words beginning with each letter in the word *dictionary. Example:* dog, igloo, cheer, tank, Indian, orange, navy, apple, rhino, yam.

DIORAMAS. Dioramas are miniature scenes that depict an event or an idea. They are frequently made with empty shoe boxes. Dioramas may be used in all subject matter areas.

After the students have obtained a box, they may use a variety of methods to complete the project. They may use chalk, tempera, water colors, oils, pastels, colored pencils, pens, markers, or construction paper to decorate the project.

Miniature figures may be made with buttons, toothpicks, clothespins, pipe cleaners, spools, craft sticks, wire, styrofoam, or balsa wood.

Dioramas may also be made of wood frames. These frames can be enclosed with a piece of plastic or with glass.

Some suggested topics for dioramas are:

> Betsy Ross and Her Flag
> Clocks of the Past, Present, and Future
> Simple Machines
> The Wright Brothers Do Their Thing
> Inventors and Their Inventions
> Faces Around the World
> Musicians Near and Far
> Doctor—Lawyer—Indian Chief (occupations)
> Caveman Art

DISCIPLINE.   Discipline is: a problem for teachers.
                                   a problem for students.
                                   a result of experience.
              Discipline is not: synonymous with punishment.
                                  impossible to achieve.

The following suggestions may help to define and erase some problems with discipline. They may work with certain classes at certain times. They are not cure-all's.

1. Divorce a student's behavior in relationship to the grades he receives.
2. Treat all the students fairly.
3. Put yourself in the student's place. Imagine how it would feel to be in a classroom again.
4. Challenge the students with assignments.
5. Use periodic student conferences as a means of solving problems before they start.
6. Overlook certain behaviors and misbehaviors.
7. Use the concept of feedback to improve the instruction of your students.
8. Be aware of the background of each child.
9. Be consistent in your handling of behavior problems.
10. Make the students aware of your acceptance level in the areas of noise and behavior.

11. Use the affective domain of education. Deal with the students on a human level.
12. Use nonverbal communication.

DIVERSITY. Diversity and variety provide spice for the classroom. All people get bored doing the same things in the same way every day.

1. Change the opening exercises daily by having the students lead the class.
2. Change the teaching schedule periodically. Rotate subjects from morning to afternoon. Have some quiet times and some that are not exactly quiet.
3. Vary your approaches to instruction. Try using different audio and visual devices.
4. Have the students teach a lesson to the class. Play the role of a student while the student plays the role of a teacher.
5. Constantly evaluate and seek methods to improve.
6. Read stories to the students instead of always having them read to you.
7. Have round-table discussions as an alternative approach to achieving solutions to problems.
8. Use the books in the library to teach reading.

Be aware of ruts and avoid them if possible.

DO IT YOURSELF. These activities are for the teacher to do. They will give you brief, helpful hints for improving your class and your method of instruction.

1. Set up a card catalog system that will list the books, games, tapes, autio-visual equipment, and instructional aids you have in your classroom.

2. Organize a picture file for bulletin boards and class projects. Mount them or put them in large folders. Organize them by subjects, seasons, or alphabetical order. Devise your own system.

3. Organize your ditto masters, worksheets, and supplemental materials so you can easily find them when needed. Loose-leaf binders may also be used.

4. Keep a card file or notebook of unusual and exciting lesson material for use when you need a new or creative idea.

5. Make a collection of art projects. List the materials required for the project and the procedures.

These suggestions are just a few of the things you can do by yourself to make your teaching more effective.

DOLLAR BILL INQUIRY. This activity applies the process of inquiry to a dollar bill. The same process may be applied to arrowheads, ancient tools, or any other hands-on object. A discussion should be held before, during, and after this activity.

Directions for the Students:
You have been on an archaeological expedition to an ancient historical site. While unearthing a dig, you have discovered this artifact (a dollar bill). Your task is to look at the artifact and describe it. Tell about the people who made it.

The only rule is that you must form your conclusions only from what you are able to read and interpret from the material on the bill itself. You must observe. Don't tell what you know through some other way.

Here are some possible responses to the dollar bill inquiry:

numerical system	paper	two languages
women (U.S. treasurer)	calendar (dates)	United States
	technology	olive leaves (peace)
"Eye"	trade	birds
banking system	religion	keys
arrows (war)	ink	grain products
architecture	engraving	government
men	pyramids	farming
scales		

DRAMATICS. Dramatics provides the students and the teachers an opportunity to enjoy the learning process.

1. Select a theme or topic—ecology, for example.

2. Write a play, have the students write a play, or find a play. A good source is *A Change of Hearts* by Kenneth Koch. Others are *Instructor*, *Teacher*, and other professional magazines.

3. Organize the class into committees—scenery, costumes, director, and cast committees.

4. Modify the play for the specific abilities and needs of your class. Re-write as needed or delete items not appropriate.

5. Have open tryouts. Don't pre-select the best students for the parts.

6. Be sure that all students participate in some way—either on stage or behind the scenes.

7. Decide whether the play will be only for your class, for your grade, or for the entire school.

8. Practice.

The benefits derived from plays may include self-assurance, confidence, experience before an audience, and appreciation of the arts.

DROPOUTS.   Dropouts occur at all levels of education. What can a teacher do to prevent dropouts from his classroom?

1. Use the cumulative records carefully and effectively. Look for patterns in absence, attitudes, and problems in subject-matter areas. Read the previous comments and talk with the teachers.

2. Visit the home. A problem with a child may be settled when you understand the home background. You will see the child in a different light.

3. Set up a conference time with the students. Make yourself available to talk with them on a one-to-one basis.

4. Set realistic, achievable goals for the students to accomplish. They must suceed at school. Use learning contracts.

5. Ask for help. Use the guidance counselor, the school psychologist, and the child study team.

6. Analyze your methods in terms of meeting the individual and specific needs of each child. (See INDIVIDUALIZATION.)

DRUG EDUCATION.   Drug education is frequently ignored in some schools. "We're too busy teaching reading, writing, and math to do that." Familiar?

Drug education is a basic part of the social science or the science program as well as part of the health education program.

At the primary level of instruction, the students should be given intensive instruction in the areas of:

1. The proper use of medication.
2. Respect for medicines, and household detergents, etc.
3. Avoiding taking pills from friends or strangers.
4. The values of good health.
5. The purpose and jobs of doctors and other health personnel.

These basic areas can be developed into several units of instruction. More in-depth topics will be handled at the elementary level.

Some topics for instruction and discussion of drug education at the intermediate level are:

1. History of drugs.
2. Use, abuse, and effects of drugs.
3. Social pressures faced by students.
4. Alcohol and the effects upon the body.
5. Smoking and its effects.
6. Prescriptions.

Many meaningful activities may be developed to teach the units on drug education:

1. Have a role-playing session, in which the students play the roles of drug users, drug pushers, narcotics agent, parents of a user, pharmacist, or the judge at a trial.
2. Make charts and displays about the use of drugs.

3. Hold "rap" sessions with the students.

4. Draw pictures of people in pain and the drugs that will help them to become better.

5. Have the students write reports that list the reasons for using drugs.

6. Observe commercials to see what pressures are used to make people buy various products. (See ADVERTISE-MENTS.)

7. Make a modern dictionary of drug-related terms.

8. Find out more about your local drug prevention units.

9. Have each student write letters to local, state, and federal agencies for information.

10. Invite the local or state police to speak to the students about drug education.

11. Make bulletin boards and collages with advertise-ments.

12. Make a scrapbook of newspaper articles dealing with drug-related crimes and events.

13. Invite the school nurse to visit with your class.

Develop similar activities on the subjects of alcohol and smoking.

— the fifth letter of the alphabet; a letter that means effort; and for education—the name of the game.

ECOLOGY (ENVIRONMENTAL EDUCATION). Ecology may be defined as the relationship between and among plants, animals, air, soil, and water. Man may also be included in the definition.

Some basic environmental concepts at the elementary level include:

1. Man must conserve natural resources.
2. Natural resources are affected by man.
3. Pollution is caused by man and also by nature.
4. Nature's cycles help to maintain life.
5. An area's ecology is in a constant state of change.
6. Four basic types of pollution are air, water, land, and sound.
7. Pollution can be controlled.
8. Animals and plants adapt to the environment.
9. Erosion has many causes and creates many problems.
10. Individual action may help solve problems.

Some basic activities that can help to develop the concepts follow:

Nature:

1. Make several collections of leaves, rocks, insects, shells, and flowers. Label them. Display them in the classroom.

2. Make a nature scrapbook with pictures or drawings of natural scenes. One section could be titled "Before and After." This would show nature before and after pollution.
3. Develop several art projects using leaves and other natural objects. *Examples:* leaf prints, stone sculpture, branch figures, or a miniature log cabin.
4. Study a micro-community. Block off a section of grass near the playground. Keep track of all living things, stones, and garbage within the area. Check the section periodically during the year to observe any changes. (See PLANTS.)

Air Pollution:

1. Take pictures of various sources and results of air pollution. Set up a display.
2. Keep track of the dirt and soot on the windows in your classroom.
3. Make a record of diseased and dead trees along highways and city streets. Develop a plan of action.
4. Find pictures of people and animals enjoying the fresh air. Superimpose pictures of pollution.
5. Check the exhaust pipes of several cars. Put a dab of petroleum jelly on a sheet of white filter paper. Place this near the exhaust for a minute, then observe the results.
6. Observe smokestacks and write letters to the people responsible for air pollution.
7. Inspect homes for the effects of pollution. Some you may find are cracking paint, rust, and ruined siding.
8. Do a research project on temperature inversions.
9. Hold a round-table discussion based on the topic of "Should Open Fires Be Banned?"
10. Design a pollution-free factory for the future.

Land:

1. Write a story entitled "Every Litter Bit Hurts." Illustrate it.

2. Take a picture of a natural scene. Paste litter on it. Describe the new picture.
3. Clean up an area along the side of a road or highway. Keep a record of the types of litter found in the area.
4. Keep track of the garbage in your classroom. Find out how much each person contributes to the total.
5. Invent a new way to recycle trash.
6. Set up a recycling program in your classroom.
7. Set up an experiment with two plants. Keep one near a factory and the other inside your classroom. Compare.
8. Make a list of some of the things found in a garbage dump.
9. Find out what recycled goods can be bought at the local stores.
10. Trace the history of a car from steel mill to recycling plant. Become the car and tell its story.
11. Write letters to plastic companies about recycling.

Water:

1. Keep a newspaper record of oil spills in the water. If you can, locate the cause of each.
2. What would happen if the world's water were suddenly to become polluted? Write about it.
3. "Water, water, everywhere, nor any drop to drink . . . ." Make a list of the ways in which we use and abuse water.
4. What state, local, or federal laws protect our water? Write letters to officials to find out.
5. Find out what procedures are used to prevent oil spills. Write a letter to a major oil company.
6. Become a fish sick from polluted water. Tell your story.
7. Write a letter to the local sewage treatment plant to learn more about its operation.
8. Take several samples of water from the area. Observe them. Test for chlorine or other chemicals.
9. Do some research on the Great Lakes and what has happened to them.

10. Make a chart of ways to prevent water pollution. Send this to the Environmental Protection Agency.

Sound (Noise Pollution):

1. Tape record the sounds in front of the school, in the cafeteria, and on the playground. Play the tape for the class.
2. Have an hour of silence during the day. Write how it felt to be quiet for that period of time.
3. Go outside for a mini-field trip. Say nothing. Write down all the sounds you hear. Determine the source of each sound.
4. Find out what a muffler is on a car. Write a letter to an automobile manufacturer to find out.
5. Keep a record of the kinds of cars and trucks that pass in front of the school. Which cars are the loudest? What can be done to alleviate the problem?
6. Put on a mask and ear plugs. Tell how this feels.
7. What can you do as an individual to curb noise pollution? Make a list of suggestions.
8. Write several comparisons: "as loud as. . .," "as quiet as. . . ." Illustrate them.
9. Hold a panel discussion to determine the effects of loud rock music on hearing.
10. Sing and talk to plants to see how this will affect their growth. Keep records.

Inside the Classroom:

1. Write letters to legislators asking them to inform you of their positions in regard to pollution and the environment.
2. Use milk cartons for art projects and experiments.
3. Use a lunch box instead of a paper bag, or re-use the paper bags.
4. Recycle paper in the classroom. Use both sides.
5. Make compost piles near the classroom.
6. Save greeting cards and recycle them.

7. Use pencils until they can no longer be used.
8. Use the library instead of buying books. Bring in old books and repair them.
9. Make your own gifts for special events and holidays.
10. Recycle crayons.

The students may suggest many more activities dealing with environmental education. Add to these lists.

ECONOMICS EDUCATION. Economics education is frequently ignored and usually feared. It involves the basics of economics as applied to the classroom.

Topics include currency, production, distribution of goods, products, and the workings of government.

Here are some sample activities that can be done with students:

Money:

1. What is money? Research the history of money. Make a chart comparing the various types of money in the past.
2. Make a list of reasons why people need money.
3. Find out more about credit cards. Design your own.
4. Make a chart comparing the currencies of different countries.
5. Find out what "good as gold" means.
6. Trace the travels of a dollar bill.
7. Write a story about "The Dollar That No One Wanted."
8. Design some money for the future.
9. Keep track of the money that you spend for a whole month.

Production:

The assembly line process may be taught in the classroom by having students work on a project with an assembly line procedure.

One suggestion is to put together a class magazine or newspaper. Each child is given a specific task to accomplish. The concept of "specialization" may also be introduced. Another possible project would be to make a stuffed animal from cloth and rags.

If permissible—and if a market is available—the students could sell the product of their works.

Other Topics Related to Economics:

1. *Foods and marketing:* Visit the local supermarket to find out more about foods and food processing.
2. *The stock market:* Use the newspaper to learn more about fractions. Keep track of several stocks for a period of time.
3. Follow the prices and production of oil and gas.
4. Find out more about the imports and exports of the United States. Make a chart comparing them.
5. Research the effects of weather on farm products.
6. Develop several product-testing experiments.
7. Design a product of the future. Give it a name and tell how it was made. (See CAREER EDUCATION and ADVERTISEMENTS.)

EMOTIONS.

"Help Me!!"
"Let's get this class QUIET!!"

Emotions and feelings are a part of the classroom.

1. Express your feelings to the students. If their talking really bothers you, tell them so.
2. Use statements such as:
School is _____
I wish I could _____
to learn more about the students. Have them complete the unfinished sentences. (See PROJECTIVE TECHNIQUES.)

3. Change your voice inflection with moods. (See ACTION WORDS.)
4. Have the students keep diaries to be shared with you only if *they want* to share them.
5. Hold frequent rap sessions. (See MAGIC CIRCLE.)

ENRICHMENT ACTIVITIES.   Enrichment activities are needed when students have completed the basic requirements as established by the teacher and the curriculum. The activities may be individual, for small groups, or for the entire class.

Mathematics:

1. Develop and use tangrams—geometric shapes used to make squares. They were developed by the Chinese.
2. Have the students make puzzles for other students.
3. Write some original world records. Publish a book of your world records. Each student's work should be included.
4. Make up a new numeration system. Do a research project on the ancient numeration systems.
5. Make a collection of mathematics oddities and write curious problems with them. (See MATHEMATICS.)

Language Arts:

1. Write and illustrate an original book. Place it in the library.
2. Have the students develop an interest center for the class. (See INTEREST CENTERS.)
3. Write a letter to a famous sports figure or movie person.
4. Make up an original game with instructions and board.
5. Write an original story based on the pattern:

   Why the (camel) (tiger) got his (hump) (stripes) etc.

6. Write and illustrate a tall tale.

(See CREATIVE WRITING and POETRY.)

Science:

1. Present an independent experiment to the class.
2. Illustrate a man of the past, the present, and the future. Write an accompanying report.
3. Classify objects on a science table in several different ways.
4. Write a story about the causes of seasons.
5. Work on models of plants or animals.
6. Pick one of the senses and develop an in-depth project.
7. Make a papier mache project related to the topic. (See ANIMALS and PLANTS.)

Social Studies:

1. Make a salt, flour, and water map of an area.
2. Make a diorama of a given topic. (See DIORAMAS.)
3. Develop a paper of the past or a newspaper of the future. (See NEWSPAPERS.)
4. Analyze today's people as if you were looking back after 100 years.
5. Make a set of transparencies to supplement the lessons. (See TRANSPARENCIES.)

Creative Arts:

1. Find some appropriate music to illustrate the background for a story in reading.
2. Illustrate the story.
3. Make up a series of questions and answers so that the answers are part of a record. Tape record this.
4. Make some puppets and a stage.

Enrichment activities should be available to the students at all times. They will provide the needed motivation for all the students.

ETHNIC STUDIES. Ethnic studies involve the various cultures of the world. The curriculum may be divided into several concept areas. Activities may be developed as a basis for teaching the concepts.

Concept: All people are interdependent.

1. Discuss the role of families. What different types of families are found throughout the world? How are they alike? How are they different?

2. Make picture of houses throughout the world—igloos, grass huts, cliff houses, etc. Compare.

3. Compare schools and the subjects taught in each. What different languages do you find?

4. Different groups of people have communities that are different. Research some rituals.

5. Have an International Day. Each student represents a different country and different culture. Serve foods that are particular to each country.

Concept: All people are alike.

1. Foods: All man needs food. Study the foods of other cultures.

2. Clothing: Draw or find pictures of various modes of dress.

3. Life purpose: Make a list of some of the goals of all people.

4. Recreation: Research some special games of Africa, Spain, Germany, and other countries.

Concept: People are different.

1. Cuturally: Define culture. Make a list of the special characteristics of Asiatic and Western cultures.

2. Emotionally: Are all people friendly? Why do people react differently in different situations?

3. Physically: Racial differences may be discussed here. What is melanin? Why are Indians called "Redskins"? What is a "paleface"?

Concept: People are affected by environment.

1. Weather: Discuss changes in climate and weather on the behavior and life styles of people.

2. Food.
3. Clothing.
4. Occupations.
5. Make a chart comparing the foods, clothing, and occupations of different cultures.

After these basic studies, you can do the following:

1. Make detailed reports about famous people of Afro-American, Spanish-American, or other descent.
2. Make several art projects illustrating "It's a Small World."
3. Write letters to other countries.
4. Obtain posters and souvenirs from other areas.

ETYMOLOGY. Etymology is the scientific study of the history and origin of words. This can be extremely challenging to both the teacher and the student.

The dictionary, encyclopedia, and books of word origins will help in these activities.

Some words come from foreign countries and have meanings in another language. Example—Florida means "flowered" in Spanish; Colorado means "red" in Spanish.

Other words were named after people. The Tommy gun was named after its inventor—Thompson. The zeppelin was named after Count Von Zeppelin.

Others resulted as a contraction. Motel is a shortened form of "motor hotel."

Other words and expressions reflect the cities of their origin—for example, the "frankfurter" was named for the city in Germany where it was first made. "Mind your P's and Q's" came as a result of British innkeepers minding the pints and quarts of the customers drinking ale.

This activity sheet may be done with the aid of a good dictionary. Some clues are provided.

Try to find the origins and meanings of these words:

Word	Clue	Your Guess	Meaning and Origin
hamburger	city in Germany		
assassin	hashish		
rosewood	color		
piedmont	mountain		
hemisphere	"ball"		
graffiti	tele*graph*		
quicksilver	fast moving		
centipede	*cent*ury		
Los Angeles	not devilish		
Bridgeton	town with —		
swordfish	blade		
lunatic	lunar		
gatling gun	man's name		
tenpenny	money		
jellyfish	shakes like—		

Add more to this list. Modify the activity to meet the needs of the class. (See **VOCABULARY**.)

EVALUATION. Several ways to evaluate student progress follow:

1. Establish a checklist to evaluate the students' work while they are working on a project. The list should include student interest, independence of the workers, quality of the final product, and the effort of the student based upon his ability.

2. Student self-evaluation. During and after a report, project, or other activity, have the student evaluate his own progress. At the primary level, the student may draw a smile

face if he is pleased, a frown if he is not pleased, and a face with a question mark if he is not sure. At the intermediate level, the students may complete unfinished sentences:

(1) I was pleased with . . . .
(2) I was not very happy about . . . .
(3) If I could change something about my work, it would be .
(4) Next time I do a project, I will . . . .

Students may also keep a daily diary to tell how they feel about their progress.

3. Conferences. During the course of a project, hold a conference with the students to discuss problems. Offer suggestions to help them. Have the students also offer suggestions.

4. Instead of tests, use other devices to evaluate. Some of these alternative ways include student-made bulletin boards, oral reports, written reports, art projects, letter-writing activities, plays, and your own personal opinion.

EXERCISES. Hup—2—3—4! Exercises are needed—for young and old—for teacher and student.

In addition to the regular physical education program, you can have some exercises within the classroom.

When the students have been sitting for a long period of time and are getting restless, take ten minutes out to:

1. Bend and stretch.
2. Run in place for a minute.
3. Have deep breathing exercises.
4. Imagine you are touching the ceiling and the floor at the same time. Stretch.
5. Touch both walls of the room at the same time.
6. Do some head twisters.

These exercises will help to circulate the blood to the students' brains and will provide a needed break during the day.

EXPERIMENTS Science is a subject which must be *done*—not read about.

In order to be effective, experiments:

1. Must be challenging to the students.
2. Should contain the planning of both the teacher and the students.
3. Must have a definite purpose.
4. Must be modified to meet the needs of the students.
5. Should be done according to the scientific method.
6. Should result in learning.

— the sixth letter of the alphabet; a grade that means failure; and for feelings—which should be a part of education.

FEELINGS.   Feelings can be taught in the classroom.

1. Set up a "feelings" center. Place a series of different feelings on index cards. Have the students draw a picture to match the words. Describe the pictures. *Examples:* "I feel tired."—"I feel hungry."—"I feel angry."

2. Develop a picture file of emotion-laden pictures. On the back of each picture, make a list of several leading questions. Have the students list words that describe the pictures. Place the pictures in a folder and allow the students to see the reactions of others.

3. Have the students draw pictures of you with a sad, a happy, a grumpy, and a tired face. Mount these and laminate them. Put one of the appropriate faces on your desk each day to indicate your mood. If the grumpy face appears too often, change it.

4. To determine the students' feelings toward their classmates, use a sociogram. It is a device that determines the popularity of the students.

Tell the students that they are going to have a party. They are to list three students in the class whom they will invite and one whom they would not invite. Tally the results.

This technique will show you who is the most popular student and who is a social isolate. Do this several times during the year to see if any changes have taken place.

FIELD TRIPS. Field trips provide the students with outside-the-classroom experience. They are *not* a waste of time and money.

Guidelines for field trips include:

1. Establish objectives for the trip. Have definite educational goals that will be attained during the trip.
2. Establish standards of behavior for the students. This can be done in a democratic way.
3. Confirm the trip in writing, allowing yourself sufficient time for problems that may develop.
4. Re-confirm the arrangements by phone.
5. If appropriate, contact parents for help with the trip.
6. Discuss with the students the objectives and activities of the trip, and what they should hope to learn from it.
7. Provide follow-up materials for the students. The writing of thank-you letters is one of the activities that should be included.
8. Review the lessons—both planned and incidental—that happened on the trip.
9. Devise a checklist to be sure everything is provided. Some considerations in this area are transportation, costs, eating facilities, lavatory facilities, permission notices, and activities before, during, and after the trip.
10. After the trip, sit down and review. Write some recommendations for the trip next year.

FILMS. Educational films provide the teachers with a supplemental instructional tool. It is one media that is effective at all levels of instruction.

Some unusual ways to use films in the classroom are:

1. Run the film projector without sound. You can narrate the film. The students can also narrate the film. This can be a challenging project.

2. Tape record a series of questions for the students. As the film is played without sound, play the tape recorder. Discuss the questions.

3. Run the film projector without the picture. Have the students imagine the types of pictures that would accompany the narration. Then show the film and compare the comments with the film.

4. Play the film backward. Have the students put the sequence of events in the proper order.

5. Obtain a used 16 mm. film from the public library. Bleach the film in household bleach. Rinse and dry. Use marking pens to create designs on the film. Record a narration or music to accompany the film. Blank film may also be obtained through the audio-visual distributor.

6. Have the students write letters to the producers of films to obtain more information about the film.

Free films may be obtained from the telephone company, oil companies, and many local industries. Insurance companies also provide similar services. The usual procedure is that you pay the return postage.

The evaluation form shown in Figure 3 will help to improve the use of films in the classroom.

---

16 mm. Film Evaluation

Title of film _____ Number _____

Source _____ Color _____ Black/white _____

Time _____ Grade level _____ Date of film _____

Related topics for discussions _____

Special vocabulary _____

Related (follow-up) lessons _____

Reaction of students/teacher _____

Cost of film _____ Rental fee _____

(Additional Comments)

_____

_____

FIGURE 3: **Film Evaluation Form**

S. Filmstrips should be previewed; are used to ...velop, or culminate units of study; and can be an ...of a learning center.

...ke your own. . .

1. Commerically prepared blank filmstrip is available through audio-visual or camera stores. Use pens, pencils, or special overhead pens to create your own filmstrips.

2. Have a roll of 35 mm. film developed—*without* using a camera. Instruct the dealer not to cut the film. Bleach the film with household bleach. Rinse and dry. Use pens and create your own filmstrip.

3. Use a 35 mm. camera with slide film. Turn the camera to a vertical position rather than a horizontal one. Take the pictures in the sequence you would like. Have the film developed— without cutting the film. The filmstrip can be used with a filmstrip projector. (See SLIDES.)

FLANNELBOARDS. Flannelboards may be made rather inexpensively.

Use a 2′ x 3′ board or a size that is appropriate for your needs. Cover the board with flannel. Glue, tack, or staple the flannel onto the board.

Make letters, numbers, or pictures from small pieces of flannel.

Flannelboards may be used in all subject matter areas. (See Figure 4.)

FLASHCARDS. Flashcards may be purchased locally for a minimal price. Students may also make their own sets of cards in the areas of language arts (vocabulary) or in mathematics (number facts).

Other areas that lend themselves to the development of flashcards are social studies and science.

The cards may have a question on one side and the answer on the other. This will give a positive and immediate reinforcement to the student. (See Figure 5.)

FIGURE 4: Flannelboard

This sample of flashcard can be applied to all states or countries. The answer to the question (*Trenton*) would appear on the back of the card.

Other shapes that could be used are triangles, shapes of fruits and vegetables, and shapes of people.

Appropriate questions would then be developed.

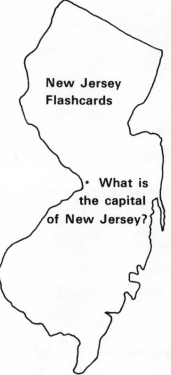

New Jersey Flashcards

* **What is the capital of New Jersey?**

FIGURE 5: Flashcard

FOLKLORE. Folklore includes the customs, beliefs, and traditions passed down throughout the years. Myths, legends, fables, and tales are all a part of a country's folklore.

Folklore has a place in the elementary classroom.

1. Discuss the life, dress, and songs of the American cowboy. Put on a play about the modern cowboy.

2. Make a list of the customs that have been handed down since colonial times.

3. Set up a table display of assorted books and pamphlets about such people as Paul Bunyan, John Henry, Ulysses, Rip Van Winkle, and Davy Crockett.

4. Write an original folk tale with your students. Illustrate it and make it into a book for the library.

5. Make a list of expressions and figures of speech that have a basis in folklore: "Achilles' heel," "the strength of Hercules," or "Atlas has the world on his shoulders."

6. Listen to some modern folk songs. Compare them to the songs of long ago.

7. Keep a list of vocabulary words that have historical origins—"cereal" from Ceres, etc.

8. On a map, locate famous folk heroes such as Johnny Appleseed or Casey Jones. Locate Blackbeard's treasure if you can.

9. Make a folklore newspaper. (See NEWSPAPER.)

10. Do an in-depth project about a famous mythological person or place. *Examples:*

Apollo	Diana	Jupiter	Mercury	Pluto
Atlas	Hercules	Mentor	Neptune	Trojan Horse
Centaur	Isis	Midas	Olympus	Unicorn

FOOD.

The shortest path to a student's brain is through his stomach.

Harold I. Cotler

In many social studies and science units, food can be incorporated into the classroom. It also fits into the language arts area as well as career education.

Example: In a study of a country, the culminating activity can be a dinner. In order to plan a dinner, total cooperation of the students is necessary.

The students are involved in the planning process in all stages of the activity's development. They can suggest foods for the dinner. The can prepare the food, serve it, eat it—and work on the clean-up committee.

Some examples of classroom projects centering around specific foods are:

Florida	citrus day
Mexico, Spain	fiesta

Indians	Indian food day—corn, succotash, etc.
United Nations	international foods
New England	maple syrup, seafood
New Jersey	dairy foods
Hawaii	luau
Italy	assorted specialties
Colonial history	venison, old-fashioned breads, etc.

Use your units and your ingenuity to help the students remember the subject. For a lesson in creative writing, the students can imagine how a pretzel feels—and then eat one.

FUTURE.   The study of the future can be relevant to today's students.

Here are several ways to involve the students in a study of the future:

1. Read sections of *1984* by George Orwell. Discuss the meaning of the sections with the students.

2. Discuss the movie "2001." Make a model spacecraft of the future.

3. Make a chart comparing life 100 years ago to life of today. Some topics are dress, transportation, health, careers, and customs.

4. Design a man of the future. Make a large model for the class.

5. Write letters to a computer company to find out more about how man works with computers.

6. Do a research project about robots.

7. Observe cartoons and shows on television. How many of the cartoon ideas are possible in our future?

8. If possible, obtain old Flash Gordon comic books. How many of the dreams have come true today?

9. Tape record a trip into the future.

10. Design a future city, and build a model of it with balsa wood. Describe it.

— the seventh letter of the alphabet; for gentle, which teachers must be; and for goals which must be achieved.

GAMES. Games must be used in effective ways in schools Students learn through play. Games provide learning for life. They provide practice in mathematics, language, reading, and thinking skills. Socializing processes also are developed.

Some games for classroom use follow:

1. WHO AM I? (Primary-Intermediate).

Give the students the clues one at a time. Have them guess the object or animal.

1. I am a reptile.
2. My skeleton is outside my body.
3. I can stretch my neck in and out.
4. I live in the water.
5. I lay eggs.
6. My shell is dark and yellow.
7. Don't put your hand near my mouth or I may snap it off.
— WHO AM I? (*Snapping turtle.*)

Modify the game for other animals, places, people, events, or occupations. Make the clues appropriate to your grade level.

2. WHAT'S MISSING? (Primary-Intermediate).

Take a set of flash cards or picture cards. Place 20 of them on the chalkboard in a random fashion.

Have one child leave the room for a minute. Remove one card. Ask the child to guess which card is missing.

This game will help to improve the powers of concentration.

3. WHAT'S MY LINE? (Primary-Intermediate).

Select three students to portray a famous person, event, or object. Have the other students in the class guess their identity.

4. MAKE YOUR OWN GAME.

Materials: felt remnants, assorted pictures, white glue, and game board (checkerboard).

Cover the game board with assorted pictures.

Make up a set of rules and regulations for the game. The students may also make up the rules.

See the Aloha Game (Figure 6.)

Directions for the game:

Toss a checker onto the game board. If it lands on an object, describe the object in a complete sentence. If it lands on a letter, tell something about Hawaii that begins with that letter. If it lands on a blank space, throw again.

GEOGRAPHY. Geography is generally integrated within the framework of the social studies curriculum. Many concepts are developed in the study of geography. Some of these concepts follow.

The Earth's Surface:

1. Make a diorama to show the layers of the earth's surface and also one to illustrate the layers in the atmosphere.
2. Do a project based on the ozone and its effects upon the atmosphere.
3. Define *biosphere*. Relate the word origin to "bionics," "biology," and "biochemistry."
4. Make a salt, flour, and water map of a mountain and a valley.

FIGURE 6: The Aloha Game

5. Make a list of the appropriate vocabulary words. Make a chart with the word, its meaning, and a picture.

Water:

1. Write reports about the various oceans and life in the oceans.
2. Look up the history of a specific ocean—Balboa and "the Specific Pacific."
3. Trace a body of water (a river) from its source.
4. Make a chart comparing a lake to a stream and bay, etc.
5. Write a story entitled "Water, Water, Everywhere."

Climate:

1. Define *weather* and *climate*. Compare and contrast them.
2. Make a list of the factors affecting the climate.
3. Find the Trade Winds, the Gulf Stream, and the Labrador Current. What bodies of land do they affect?
4. How would the climate of the earth change if there were no sun? Write a report on this subject.

Natural Resources:

1. Explain why man is sometimes called our greatest natural resource.
2. Write letters to various energy-producing companies and oil companies to find out more about their efforts to save the natural resources. (See ECOLOGY.)
3. Set up a recycling project in the classroom.
4. Hold a round-table discussion to determine if our resources are unlimited or limited.

Population:

1. Place the following question on a map of the world: "Why do people settle here?" Place a sheet of paper

beneath the question and ask the students to answer it in terms of one specific part of the world.

2. On a map, locate the densely populated areas in your city, state, or section of the United States.
3. Do a research project about the origins of the people in America.
4. Design a house that will hold 100 people. Describe it.

World Regions:

1. Discuss Columbus' traveling west to reach the East.
2. Do an in-depth project about the Middle East. Why is this area a problem one?
3. Work with a map or globe to determine the Eastern and Western Hemispheres. (See MAPS.)
4. Who belongs to the Western World? Why?
5. Compare the Asian Culture to the American culture.

Directions:

The concept of longitude and latitude is developed at different levels of difficulty. Parallels and meridians are also discussed. (See MAPS.)

Cities:

1. Why do cities usually start along a river? Make a survey through letters to find out which cities had their start in this way.
2. Make a map of the major cities around you. What are some of the problems in the cities?
3. Write a letter to your local planning board to find out more about your city.
4. Design a transportation system for the 21st century.

Earth-Sun Relationships:

1. Compare rotation to revolution.
2. Make a model of the earth with a balloon and papier mache. Make a model of the sun in the same way.

3. Find out how hot the sun is. What are sunspots? (See WEATHER.)
4. Why is Alaska called the Land of the Midnight Sun?
5. Write a detailed report about *night* and *day*.

Games can help to make the study of geography more enjoyable for the students.

1. GUESS THE STATE GAME (Intermediate).

On an outline map of the United States, have the children put a number in each state. (Alabama—1; Alaska—2.)

Select three students to observe the map for three minutes. Then, after one student selects a number, the three students in front of the class must guess the state. If they don't, they must change places with another student. Modify this game for your own class.

2. WHAT COUNTRY AM I?

Do a research project about a country. Include the basic facts about the country on a worksheet. Have the students guess the country and verify their guess with an atlas, encyclopedia, or other reference book.

Game 1:

My highest point is 568 feet above sea level. I am also on sea level. People buy objects with kroner. I have a Parliament and Prime Minister to help run the country. Many farms and lakes are located within my borders. I have five million people. My area is 16,629 square miles. I export bacon, ham, and cheese. King Harald united me in 950. I am also a kind of pastry.
WHO AM I?   (Denmark)

Game 2:

My flag colors are red, white, and blue. My language is one of the great languages of the world. My population is 52,000,000 and my area is 211,208 square miles. My main products are fruit, livestock, fish, and dairy products. I celebrate a special day on

July 14. My money is almost like my name. I have a President
and a Prime Minister. Come to me and visit the Louvre.
                WHO AM I?   (France)

Make up your own games like this. The students can also
make up some once they have learned how to do it.

GIFTED CHILD. The gifted child is sometimes ignored
because he is doing well in school. He may be intellectually,
physically, artistically, or musically gifted. He has a special
talent or ability.

What can a teacher do with and for the gifted child?. . .

1. Provide one-to-one instruction for him.

2. If he is capable of going ahead faster in reading or
mathematics, make arrangements to have him work in another
grade.

3. Use him to tutor other students. This will help both
students.

4. Use the child's special talents to enhance his self-
concept. Have a one-child art display or talent show. Give the
student an opportunity to act in a leadership role in committees.

5. Use learning contracts whenever possible. Give the
child a large responsibility in establishing the goals and
materials for the contract.

6. Demand no less than he can achieve.

7. Establish independent study programs in which he
spends a specific amount of time in the learning resource center.

8. Have him develop materials for use with other students. This will give him a chance to thoroughly understand the
process of education.

9. Challenge the student with math teasers, word puzzles,
individualized spelling words, and writing of books.

10. Expand his knowledge of reference materials by making him use specific reference materials for projects. This child
can rely on books other than the encyclopedia.

GRAMMAR. Grammar instruction is probably the most difficult and least rewarding subject for both the student and the teacher. This section will deal with making grammar more meaningful to the student and less boring for the teacher.

The Parts of Speech:

Nouns—

1. Draw an abstract picture on the blackboard. Have the students describe the "thing."
2. Make a list of nouns beginning with each letter of the alphabet. Illustrate three.
3. List all the nouns in the room.
4. Select a color. Find 15 nouns that will have the same color.

Pronouns—

1. Write a story about three people. Call it "Me, Myself, and I."
2. Have the students use the newspaper and replace 15 nouns with pronouns.
3. Write a story in the first person. Find a different way to say "I." Make up another word which means "I."

Verbs—

1. Use the newspaper to find some exciting verbs. The sports section works well here.
2. Write a story entitled, "Action, Action—We Want Action!" List some exciting verbs.
3. Have each child demonstrate a verb in front of the class. Write it in a sentence.

Adjectives—

1. Make a list of adjectives that describe you.
2. How many colorful adjectives can you find in the classroom? List 50 or more.
3. Select a letter of the alphabet. Have a contest to see who can list the most adjectives beginning with that letter.

Adverbs—

1. Find ten adverbs to go with some verbs from the newspaper.
2. Listen to television and radio commercials. Record some interesting adverbs.
3. Make an "Adverb-of-the-Day" bulletin board.

Prepositions—

1. Make a chart that shows the positions of words through pictures. *Example:* "I went over my friend's house." Make the picture literal.
2. Try to write sentences without using any prepositions. What problems do you have?

Conjunctions—

1. Write five sentences. Connect each with an "and." Eliminate the "ands," and say the sentences without taking a breath.
2. Make a bulletin board entitled, "And so on, and so on. . . ." Cut out conjunctions from a newspaper or magazine.

Interjections—

1. Complete these sentences: "How it feels to get a needle __." "How it feels to get an 'A' __."
2. Write a story containing ten interjections.
3. Find some interjections during a television show. Describe the feelings that produced the interjections.

After you have developed the basic parts of speech, you can include additional activities.

GROUPING. Groups should be flexible, and should exist for fulfilling specific needs. Children who need work in specific phonic elements, for instance, should be grouped together. As soon as a group is no longer needed, it should be dissolved.

1. The child's reading group and mathematics group are based on ability. Pre-test the child and place him at the ap-

propriate level. Individualized contracts may also help to meet the student's needs.

2. Form groups around student interests. For example, a unit on machines will probably interest the boys. Allow them the freedom to work independently on the project.

3. Individualized instruction will indicate weaknesses. Small temporary groups based on weaknesses are effective. The group will disband when the needs are met.

4. Whole-class grouping is another possibility. Some students work well with the whole class. Whole-class instruction is effective when working with audio-visual aids, special programs, or lessons in which all the students are weak.

5. Students feel the need to belong to groups of all kinds. Be aware of group dynamics—the leaders and the followers.

GUIDANCE. The elementary classroom teacher has many roles. One of them is the function of a guidance counselor. Full-time guidance counselors at the elementary level are not always available for the students.

The Classroom Teacher as Counselor

1. Hold conferences with individuals on a planned basis and also on a need basis.
2. Use a sociogram to determine problems in the class and utilize the findings to help the students who are not well accepted by the class.
3. Contact parents when needed to help solve a student's problem.
4. Interpret cumulative record cards to help improve the teaching process.
5. Use all available information to develop programs for individualizing instruction. Some students must learn at the concrete level, while others can handle abstracts.
6. Have the students "teach" lessons while you behave like a student.
7. When a child misbehaves, accept his behavior and seek the causes. (See DISCIPLINE.)

8. Use test results effectively. Consider your judgment as well as the test results before placing a child.
9. Teach the students about careers—preparation for the future. (See CAREER EDUCATION.)

— stands for happiness; for homework, which must be evaluated; and for humanizing education.

HAWAII.   Hawaii is the fiftieth state of the Union. This entry will give several examples of how to teach your students about a state or country. The activities maybe modified to fit other parts of America or other parts of the world.

Mathematics:

1. Write original problems about Hawaii, using Hawaiian themes. Example: How much would two tons of pineapples cost if each pound was worth 29¢?
2. Use world maps and globes to measure distances from your state to Hawaii.
3. Compare the size and population of your state to that of Hawaii. Make a chart comparing the results.
4. Find out the total number of people who visit Hawaii each year.
5. Have your students write original word problems and illustrate them.

Social Studies:

1. Do a research project on the history of Hawaii. Who were some famous people in Hawaii's history?
2. As a project, report on Hawaii's famous explorer— Captain Cook, an Englishman.

3. For another project, report on one of Hawaii's most famous leaders—King Kamehameha.
4. What was the influence of outsiders on the life of the area? What would have happened if Hawaii hadn't been discovered?
5. Do a report on Hawaii's special industries, such as the sugar and pineapple industries. Bring in samples.
6. What special physical characteristics does Hawaii have? (Mountains, volcanoes, and beaches.)
7. Draw a map of Hawaii.
8. Make a salt, flour, and water map of Hawaii's eight major islands.
9. What special types of transportation are found in Hawaii? Compare to the transportation in your area.
10. Trace the origin of the people in Hawaii.

Science:

1. Develop a unit on the sea and weather. How does the sea affect the people and their industries? Compare the climate of Hawaii to that of your state.
2. Develop a unit on geology and the earth's surface. (See GEOGRAPHY and VOLCANO.)
3. Find out more about the manufacturing of products in Hawaii. What processes for food preservation were used in ancient times?
4. What special agricultural products are raised in Hawaii? How is coffee raised there? Do pineapples grow on trees? (No.)
5. What special animals and plant life are found in Hawaii?

Language Arts:

1. Write poems with a Hawaiian theme. (See POETRY.)
2. Make a travel brochure about Hawaii. Make one about your own state. Compare them.
3. Plan a trip to Hawaii. Figure out your itinerary for two weeks.

4. Write a diary about a volcano.
5. Write letters to Hawaii for information about the state. Letters may be written to the Governor, State department of tourism, or Department of Recreation.
6. Write a letter to a public school in Hawaii and try to arrange pen pals for your students.
7. Plan a meal with your students. (See FOOD.)

Music:

1. Teach your students the hula. Resource books and records are available in the school library or the public library.
2. Find some special songs that have a Hawaiian theme. Some examples are "Mele Kalikimaka" (Hawaiian Christmas) and "Tiny Bubbles" by Don Ho.
3. Make an original musical instrument. Hollow out a coconut and play it. Use bamboo to create original instruments by cutting the bamboo to different lengths.

Art:

1. Make tikis from balsa wood or plaster of Paris.
2. Make Hawaiian leis with real flowers or with flowers made of tissue paper. Seashells may also be used to make a lei.
3. Make Hawaiian dresses or grass skirts. Aloha shirts may also be made, using brightly colored cloth. Have the girls help the boys with this project.

HISTORY. History repeats itself in the classroom. Some activities that will enliven history in your classroom follow:

Columbus:

Columbus discovered America in 1492, while searching for a new ocean route to the East Indies. One group of students can play the Indians. Other characters include Columbus, King

Ferdinand, and Queen Isabella. Have the students write a mini-script. Tell the story of Columbus' discovery from the point of view of the three ships.

Colonial:

1. Make or have the students make a crossword puzzle with historical names, places, and events.

2. Oral and written reports have limitless possibilities. Have the students select a person, place, or event and present a report. These may also be tape recorded for a good effect.

3. Re-enact the signing of the Declaration of Independence. Have the students make scenery, write the dialogue, and present the event to the class during a special assembly.

4. Make a scale model of the Jamestown Colony. Re-enact the founding of the colony.

5. Research the beginnings of several colonial cities. On what geographical feature did they all settle? (River.) What are the reasons for this? Present your findings to the class.

6. Make a list of all of the problems the early colonists faced. How did they solve their problems?

7. What are some of the modern conveniences that we would not have had in colonial times?

8. John Smith of the Jamestown Colony said that if you don't work, you don't eat. Explain this. Tell how this idea would work today.

9. How would it feel to be an Indian? Tell a story about "You—the Indian."

10. Make a scale model of a plantation. Be sure to include the garden, summer house, orchard, warehouse, school, kitchen, stables, slave quarters, and the main house.

11. Draw a colonial fireplace and kitchen. Describe the differences between cooking then and now. What different types of foods were cooked in colonial times? How were the foods preserved? Share your findings with the class.

12. Build a model of a New England whaling ship. If possible, build it to scale. Use the library to find out more about the New England whaling industry.

13. Make a model of a one-room schoolhouse of colonial times. Compare it to your school. Find out the differences in the subjects taught. How were teachers in colonial times different from today's teachers?

14. Colonial punishments were different from modern ones. Look up the words "stocks" and "pillory" in a reference book. Draw these classical punishment devices.

15. Some colonial industries and occupations are still alive today. Find out more about farming, fishing, and colonial crafts.

16. Many immigrants came to America during the colonial period. Find out more about the Dutch, English, Swedish, Quakers, Puritans, and Pilgrims. Share the findings in a report to the class. You may also make a chart to compare the contributions of each group of people.

17. Have a colonial cook-in. Find several colonial recipes and cook them in the classroom. Appropriate decorations and scenery will add to the cook-in.

18. Create a time line on a bulletin board. Fill in famous historical events and birthdays of famous individuals.

19. Visit an old cemetery. Determine the origins of the people. Make gravestone rubbings and display them in the classroom.

20. Find out more about colonial crafts. Look up articles about weaving and sewing. Having a quilting bee could add to the appreciation of colonial crafts.

21. Set up a display area to examine the Constitution, the Declaration of Independence, and the Articles of Confederation. Call the display area "Freedom and You."

22. Make a time capsule and seal it. Include artifacts of the present time.

The Civil War:

Hold a round-table discussion to talk about some of the problems of the Civil War.

Locate several songs of the Civil War era. Try to find the special meanings of the songs.

Tell the story of the war from the point of view of two brothers—one fighting for the North and the other for the South.

Do a research project on slavery. (See ETHNIC STUDIES.)

Look up the article in the encyclopedia entitled "Lincoln." What was his role in the Civil War? Write a story about Honest Abe Lincoln.

Look up the meaning of *civil* in the dictionary.

World Wars:

1. Hold a discussion to determine if wars solve anything.
2. Set up a display or interest center with books, pictures, or artifacts from a war.
3. Collect stamps that portray people who were famous during times of war in our country. Design original stamps of your own.
4. Locate famous battles on a map. Draw the countries and describe the land in the areas where the battles took place.
5. Set up a display in miniature. Have the students bring in small tanks, soldiers, and buildings.

General:

1. Have students select any famous historical person and present him as a project to the class. The students may dress up as the famous person.
2. Allow the students to share with the class their stamp collections, coin collections, or toy collections from foreign countries.

3. Locate films or filmstrips that are appropriate. Be on the look-out for specials on television.
4. Write letters to various branches of the armed services for information.
5. Many pamphlets are available from the Superintendent of Documents, Washington, D.C. 20402.
6. Write letters to the Historical Commissions of other states.

HOLIDAYS. Holidays provide a multitude of learnings for both the teacher and the student. Traditional holidays find their way into the classroom. Some ways to include other themes throughout the year follow:

September: Other holidays besides the opening of school include Labor Day. Bring in several people from the world of industry and have them talk with your students. Research the history of Labor Day.

October. Besides Columbus Day and Halloween, United Nations Day is celebrated in October. Have the students dress in different ways to represent various countries of the world. Have an International Dinner. Write letters to the United Nations for more information.

November. Celebrate Election Day with an election in your classroom. The assassination of John F. Kennedy also was in November. So that your students may know about JFK, hold a special program for them.

December. Besides Christmas and Chanukah, December 7—Pearl Harbor Day—is noteworthy. Write letters to Hawaii to obtain more information. Slides are also available for purchase. Celebrate the first day of winter.

January. Chinese New Year is celebrated in January. Have a "New Years Around the World" project in which you find out how other countries celebrate the New Year.

February. Groundhog Day arrives in February. Do a research project about the groundhog. Celebrate President's Day by writing a letter to the President of the United States.

March. The Ides of March comes on March 15. Use this as an introduction to the study of Greek mythology.

April. Create your own holiday in April. Call it "Student Day." Plan a special celebration within your classroom.

May. Find out more about May Day and the Maypole. This will be a learning experience for all.

June. Flag Day provides an opportunity for the students to re-examine the history of America and its heritage.

July and *August.* These months provide time for the teacher and students to regroup and become fresh for September.

Use *The Farmer's Almanac* to find out specific events that happened throughout the years. Articles in the encyclopedias also help to provide motivating ideas. (See CALENDAR.)

HOMEWORK. Homework is not synonymous with in-class work. To be effective, homework:

> should not be used to teach new concepts.
> should reinforce previously taught skills,
> should not be excessive.
> should be novel and interesting.
> should be evaluated.
> should be returned to the student.

The quantity of homework will vary with grade level. It is up to the individual teacher to determine the needs of the students and base the homework assignments upon those needs.

Here are some novel homework assignments:

1. Have the students watch a television show to find nouns, verbs, or other parts of speech, to observe various forms of advertising techniques, to find main ideas, to look for a sequence of events, and to locate the theme or plot.

2. Have the students make up problems which reinforce skills taught in mathematics. Have them create the problems, solve them, and use them with other students in the class.

3. Have the students write a diary as an assignment. This can be used as a language arts assignment, for social studies, or for an improvement in the child's self-concept.

4. Develop a long-term project such as a scale model of a bridge or other structure. This would require both time in class and time at home to complete.

5. Have the students make a minature television screen. Write an original play for the television or adapt a television show for classroom use.

6. Assign homework from the newspaper. Have the students bring in newspapers for assignments. (See NEWS-PAPERS.)

HOMONYMS. Homonyms are words that have identical pronunciations but different meanings and spellings.

Lists of homonyms are available in dictionaries and in some thesauri.

Homonyms may be used to develop and increase vocabulary and to develop sentence sense.

One device for teaching homonyms is an interest center.

"Homonym Sam" (Figure 7) provides an idea for the teaching of homonyms. The words may be changed after a period of several weeks. The students can write sentences using the sets of homonyms.

A homonym tree may also be used. On each branch of the tree, place a set of homonyms.

Homonym hangers may also be used in the teaching process. On a series of coat hangers, place tags with string. On the tags write some different homonyms. Suspend these from the classroom lights or from the walls.

HONOR ROLL. In order to make a traditional honor roll, a student had to show outstanding achievement in the academics. Not all students made the honor roll. You can change this idea by expanding the scope of the honor roll. All students can be rewarded for achievement in school—not only in the academic subjects.

Some other honor roll categories could include Art, Music, Physical Education, Attitude, Behavior, and Creativity.

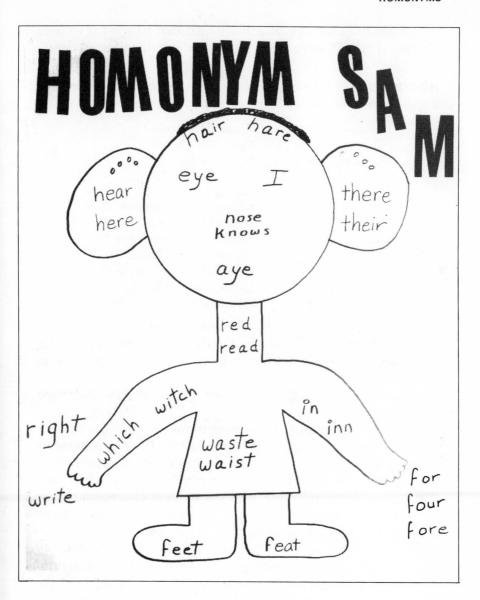

FIGURE 7: Homonym Sam

A small certificate of achievement can be mailed to each student. This will have a very positive effect upon the students.

HOROSCOPE. The future of people is sometimes read in their horoscopes. The twelve signs of the zodiac are:

Aries	March 21 - April 19
Taurus	April 20 - May 20
Gemini	May 21 - June 20
Cancer	June 21 - July 22
Leo	July 23 - August 22
Virgo	August 23 - September 22
Libra	September 23 - October 22
Scorpio	October 23 - November 21
Sagittarius	November 22 - December 21
Capricorn	December 22 - January 19
Aquarius	January 20 - February 18
Pisces	February 19 - March 20.

1. Do a research project about one of the signs.

2. Make a graph of the number of people born under each sign. Do this within the classroom or within your grade at the school.

3. Present an oral report based upon one of the stars used in the zodiac.

4. Draw some of the constellations.

5. Make up your own constellation. Give it a name, a place in the sky, and a place in the horoscope chart.

6. Put out a weekly or monthly horoscope newsletter. Write some futures for the students in your classroom.

7. Read the horoscopes in the daily newspaper. Keep track of the number of times they are correct.

8. Design a new symbol for each sign of the zodiac.

9. Take a survey among the members of a class or the students in the school to determine how many people read the horoscope in the newspaper and how many people believe in it.

10. Obtain a book which lists all the characteristics of each sign. Read them to the students. How many characteristics are true? Have the students guess why the characteristics are true.

11. Make a list of the important events that happened in the Age of Aquarius.

— stands for interest, initiative, and insight—
three qualities of a good educator.

IDEAS. There are times when teachers run out of ideas for use in the classroom. Here are some possible sources of inspiration for teachers:

advertising agencies	— Sources of advertisement techniques, possible speakers, and information.
airports	— Films, information about flights, pictures of airplanes, career education.
bakeries	— Field trips. Use cookies and cakes for creative writing.
camera shops	— Information about photography, many posters.
dog house	— Make one for the classroom. It will become a source of many ideas.
egg cartons	— Use for games, mathematics projects, storing small objects.
French fries	— This can be a class project. Have the students write directions to complete the activity. Look up the history of French fries.
gasoline stations	— Many stations have posters, career information, and free maps of the U.S.

hotels	— They will give you brochures describing the hotels and their rates. Good source of material for planning an imaginary trip.
igloo	— Make a small igloo from sugar cubes or make a large one from construction paper and cardboard boxes. Can be used to study housing and the Eskimo people.
jellyfish	— Draw a picture of a jellyfish or find one in a magazine. Make jelly with the class.
kangaroo	— Make a kangaroo for an interesting interest center. Use his pocket as a place to keep suggestions from the class.
leftovers	— Save materials and scraps from art projects to use in creating a collage.
magazines	— Use magazines to create picture files, for use in art projects, and for making activity cards.
newspapers	— Use newspapers for activities in all subjects. (See NEWSPAPERS.)
octopus	— Draw an octopus. Use each arm for a rule, question, comment, or vocabulary word.
publishing company	— These companies will help in supplying information about how a book is made and the history of books. They can be visited as a field experience. Make your own book in the classroom.
quill pen	— Make a quill pen and create an old-fashioned writing center. Compare the different styles of writing.
radio	— Listen to the radio. Make up your own radio program. If possible, ob-

	tain a recording of an old radio program.
supermarket	— The supermarket is a good place to visit on a field trip. Materials available from a supermarket include displays, signs, posters, boxes for projects, and meat trays for art projects.
television	— Instructional television may be used during the school day. It can be used to study advertising techniques, to test product claims, and to serve as motivation for creative writing.
Uncle Sam	— Design an Uncle Sam interest center. Let the students suggest another symbol for America.
vineyard	— Look up the history of grapes and wine. Why was America once called Vinland?
whales	— Illustrate and describe a whale. Compare the whale to other mammals. Make a papier mache whale.
X	— X stands for the unknown. Place an X on a sheet of paper and write or have the students write some questions.
yarn	— Have the students make yarn balls.
zoo	— Create a mini-zoo in your classroom with stuffed animals.

INDIANS.   The study of Indians provides many activities for all levels of instruction. Specific tribes or cultures may be studied. Some general topics and activities dealing with Indians are:

TOPIC	ACTIVITIES
Agriculture and Food:	
1. Use of tobacco.	1. Have an Indian Day. Make clothing and have the students dress appropriately. Eat some Indian foods.
2. Use of fish as a fertilizer.	
3. Dried meat to preserve.	
4. Succotash.	
5. Terraced farming.	2. Obtain some beef jerky and have the students eat it. Compare the various methods of food preservation.
	3. Establish several experiments with plants. Use fish as a fertilizer for some and not for others. Compare results.
	4. Make Indian tools such as stone ax.
	5. Obtain some arrowheads and use them with an inquiry approach. (See INQUIRY.)

Clothing:	
1. Skins from animals.	1. Relate to extinct or endangered species.
2. Moccasins.	2. Make some original leather products. Kits are available from arts and crafts dealers.
3. Making of cloth.	3. Set up a clothing display. Have the students make a God's Eye with yarn.

Shelter:	
Types of shelter include wigwam, wickiup, hogan, teepee, and adobe.	Make a model of each type. Use wooden tongue depressors, toothpicks. Describe each one.

Crafts and Weapons:

Items included are gourds, snowshoes, spears, tomahawks, bows and arrows, and wampum.

Activities include making necklaces, weaving, making clay pottery.

Transportation:

1. Bark and dugout canoes.

2. Snowshoes for the Northern Indians.

1. Compare to modern transportation.

2. How would an Indian of the 1600's feel about today's system of transportation?

3. Make a canoe from balsa wood.

Culture:

1. Initiation ceremonies to become a man.

2. Role of the squaw.

3. Religious beliefs.

4. Music and dance.

5. Sign language.

1. Discuss sterotypes of Indians—warrior, hunter, medicine man.

2. Compare to today's role of women.

3. Read several Indian legends and stories. Make up your own legends.

4. Do some research on Indian songs and dances. Many records are available to help.

5. Create your own sign language.

General:

Define and give examples of the following words and expressions:

arrowhead	Happy Hunting Ground	peace pipe	tomahawk
buffalo	hogan	pyramids	totem pole
ceremony	Indian summer	scalp hunter	travois
guardian spirit	maize	teepee	wampum

INDIVIDUALIZATION OF INSTRUCTION. Individualization of instruction simply means teaching each student as much as can be taught to that student—having each child work and learn at his own level.

Individualization allows the learning process to meet the needs, interests, and abilities of the child.

Some methods to use for individualizing are:

Learning Contracts (See CONTRACTS.)
Interest Centers (See INTEREST CENTERS.)
Programmed Instruction
Use of individualized reading/mathematics programs
Computer Assisted Instruction
Use of behavioral objectives (See OBJECTIVES.)

Your task is to seek and use the ways that work best for you. Or invent your own method of instruction.

INQUIRY. The process of inquiry is a method for solving problems through a systematic approach to learning.

Inquiry involves acquiring the following objectives:

1. The ability to make judgments.
2. The ability to observe systematically.
3. The ability to interpret primary and secondary source materials.
4. The ability to classify, hypothesize, and analyze.
5. The ability to form generalizations.

The model of inquiry consists of:

1. Defining the problem.
2. Developing hypotheses.
3. Collecting data and other pertinent information.
4. Evaluating and organizing data.
5. Drawing conclusions.

Some situations that lend themselves to the process of inquiry are:

1. Analyzing the causes of weather and determining the climate.
2. Organizing changes in the earth's surface.
3. Categorizing different objects.
4. Using artifacts to determine cultural traits.
5. Solving a fight in the classroom.
6. Solving ecological problems.
7. Determining the effects of overpopulation.
8. Suggesting ways to help governmental problems and world situations.
9. Finding more and better food products and food substitutes.
10. Solving the vast transportation problems that will arise in the future. (See DOLLAR BILL INQUIRY.)

INTEREST CENTERS. Interest centers are frequently called learning centers. Interest centers are composed of learning stations.

A learning station is a single, independent activity to develop a skill or ability.

A learning center consists of several learning stations and a variety of approaches in order to achieve a specific goal.

Components of a Learning Center:

Objectives: are clearly stated and clearly understood. Indicate a specific goal which can be achieved in a given period of time.

Directions: should be sequential.
should list the specifics for the center.
must be at the appropriate vocabulary level.
describe the needed materials and equipment.
should be laminated for protection.

Evaluation: should be continuous and consistent.
should include the child in the process.

should be accomplished through self-correcting devices and teacher participation.

should be done through observation, teacher-student conferences, checklists, student comments, and parent-teacher conferences.

Materials to Construct Centers:

books	magazines	rulers
cellophane tape	markers	scissors
compass	masking tape	stapler
construction paper	oak tag	staples
envelopes	paper clips	typewriter
erasers	paper fasteners	typing paper/assorted paper
felt	paper punch	wrapping paper
file folders	patterns	yardstick
glue	protractor	yarn

Tips for Making Centers:

1. Pre-plan the center before attempting to build it.
2. Build the centers in an area that does not require immediate clean-up.
3. Let the students help to make the centers.

Suggested Interest Centers
(See Figure 8)

Language Arts and Creative Writing:

"Noun Town"	pictures of nouns
"Do Your Own Thing"	study of verbs
"Call Me Indescribable"	adjectives and adverbs
"I'm Sitting on Top of the World"	prepositions
"Help! Watch Out!"	scenes that cause interjections
"Monkey Business"	pictures of monkeys
"Write On..."	pictures for creative writing
"Headliners"	newspaper headlines
"Ghosts and Ghouls"	Halloween center

(See CREATIVE WRITING and GRAMMAR.)

FIGURE 8: Interest Center

Social Studies:

"Indian Reservations"	pictures of Indian life
"My House Is Your House"	homes around the world
"America's Boosters"	famous Americans
"Our American Heritage"	pictures of American places
"Land of the Free"	Statue of Liberty
"People of the World"	world map and people

(See HISTORY.)

Science:

"Scientific Super Spy"	experiment and scientific methods
"Weather Watchers"	weather equipment/maps
"Volcano Vigil"	picture of the earth
"Out of This World"	rockets and outer space
"I Need Water, Air, and Food"	plant and animal unit

(See ECOLOGY.)

Mathematics:

"Addition—Mission Possible"	— addition problems
"Subtraction Action"	— subtraction center
"Multiplication Vacation"	— multiplication problems
"Division with Ammunition"	— division problems
"Fractured Fraction Action"	— fraction problems
"Mixed Measure Mathematics"	— word problems with measurement
"Have I Got Problems?"	— word problems
"Geometric Genius"	— geometric shapes
"A Wrecked Angle (Rectangle)"	— problems with rectangles
"Triangular Tricks"	— triangle problems
"A Real Square"	— problems with square shapes
"Decimal Decisions"	— decimal problems
"Football Figures"	— football problems
"Baseball Budget"	— baseball problems
"A Hockey Puck"	— ice hockey problems
"Metric Mission"	— metric problems

(See MATHEMATICS and METRICS.)

113

Reading:

"Folk Heroes of Today, Yesterday, and Tomorrow"
"Fairy Tales May Come True—It Happened to ME"
"Mystery of Room 10"
"Is an Autobiography the Story of a CAR?"
"Good Sports and Bad"
"Fictional Fantastic Futuristic Fun"

Music:

"I Believe in Music"	— modern records and tapes
"Music Is Love and..."	— write about music
"Do, Re, Mi........"	— the scales

(See MUSIC.)

Art:

"A Picasso—Maybe"	— create original art
"Color My World"	— different colors/paterns
"Reds, Whites, and Blues"	— historical pictures
"Mod Artist at Work"	— child creates center
"Do Your Own Thing"	— create original art

— is for joy, and jumping jacks, and jams.

JUNK. One person's junk is another person's treasure. Junk can be used to teach the students.

1. Bring in a piece of "junk." Have the students describe it. Answer the following questions:

What is it?
What is its composition?
Where was it made?
Who touched it before today?

2. Give the object a name and make it part of the class.
3. Bring in several pieces of metal from a junkyard. Have the students make a junk sculpture.
4. Make a mosaic picture from scraps of paper.
5. Keep track of the amount of trash that the class produces in a day and a week. What can be done to reduce the trash?
6. Set up a recycling program within your classroom. (See ECOLOGY.)

— is for kickball, for knowledge, and for the keys to unlock the minds of your students.

KINDERGARTEN.   Kindergarten teachers establish the future for many of the students.

Many of the activities of kindergarten teachers have applications and implications for teachers at the primary and intermediate levels.

1. *Use of concrete objects.* Many students need tactile experiences in order to reinforce abstract learnings.

2. *Share and tell (bring and brag).* All elementary students have experiences that they would like to share. At the upper levels, this becomes the current events part of the curriculum.

3. *Experience stories (charts).* This is a lesson in which the students tell a story to the teacher, and the teacher writes the story on chart paper. At the primary and intermediate levels, the charts can be the results of field trips, science experiments, or experiences at home.

4. *Use of building blocks.* Have the students make models of homes. Sugar cubes and toothpicks may be used to make the homes.

5. *Readiness skills.* Kindergarten teachers ascertain that the child is at the readiness level before progressing to the next step. Pre-test your students to be sure they are ready to progress to the next level of instruction.

6. *Read stories to students.* Part of every school day should be spent reading to the students. A good time to read stories is

just after lunch. This allows the teacher and the students to enjoy good pieces of literature or just read for pleasure.

7. *Oral communication.* Much of the language development of kindergarten students is oral. Students must be taught proper language. Choral reading is appropriate for developing effective communications skills.

8. *Physical exercises.* Many movement records and activities develop gross motor and small motor skills. (See PHYSICAL EDUCATION.)

9. *Follow the directions.* The teacher tells the students to follow a certain procedure in completing a project. The teacher demonstrates a task and the students imitate it. At the upper levels, following directions is a difficult task. Children still must be taught to follow directions.

KITS (MULTIMEDIA). Commercially prepared multimedia kits consist of two or more media presentations in a packaged product. Many kits consist of a filmstrip with a record or tape, books, booklets, transparencies, and/or ditto masters.

How to Make Your Own Multimedia Kit:

Select a given topic or unit of study. The unit may be in any subject area.

Multimedia kits may consist of the following:

Activity cards. (See TASK CARDS.)
Artifacts.
Books. Make a list of those that are available both within your classroom and from the school library.
Cassettes or tapes. Make your own tapes appropriate to the unit of instruction and also list those available in the school.
Filmstrips. Make a list of those from the school or make your own. (See FILMSTRIPS.)
Games. Make your own and also list those available. (See GAMES.)
Learning stations. (See INTEREST CENTERS.)

Lesson plans. (See LESSON PLANS.)

Pamphlets. Lists of free curriculum materials are available at public libraries and also in professional education magazines.

Pictures. Your picture file and magazines will come in handy.

Posters. Many posters are available from a multitude of sources including supermarkets, gasoline stations, and record shops.

Puzzles. Original puzzles may be made by both the students and you. (See PUZZLES.)

Records. List those available at both the public library and the school library.

Slides. Commercially prepared slides are available on many topics or you can make your own slides. (See SLIDES.)

Transparencies. (See TRANSPARENCIES.)

Vocabulary cards.

Worksheets.

The multimedia kit requires much time and effort to compile properly. but the time and effort invested will reap many rewards. The multimedia kit may be stored in a large box or filing cabinet. This organization of ideas and materials will help to effectively teach a unit of instruction. Much of the material can be used again and again.

— is for learning, living, and laughing, all of which can be part of the educational process and part of each child.

LANGUAGE ARTS. Language arts consist of the basics in oral and written communications. Individual topics are discussed throughout the book. (See ADVERTISEMENTS, ANTONYMS, BOOKS, CREATIVE WRITING, DICTIONARY, DRAMATICS, GRAMMAR, INTEREST CENTERS, LIBRARY, LISTENING, NEWSPAPERS, OUTLINING, POETRY, SPELLING, SYNONYMS, and others.)

LEARNING. Learning: is sequential.
is an active process.
is an individual process.
must use an individual's capacity and mode.

In order for a teacher to provide effective learning situations, several factors must be considered:

1. Teach children on their own level.
2. Modify your teaching techniques to meet student needs.
   a. Talk with the students as a teaching method.
   b. Show others films, filmstrips, or use tapes.
   c. Perform an experiment.
   d. Bring in pictures or concrete objects for teaching.

e. Use the inquiry process to solve problems.

f. Do an art project with others.

3. Evaluate your techniques to determine success in learning.

LESSON PLANS. A successful lesson plan file will help to improve your instruction. Lesson plans may be kept in a 5" x 8" index, in a loose-leaf binder, or in a filing cabinet.

The file should include:

the behavioral objective
special motivational devices or gimmicks
materials needed for the lesson
special vocabulary
special problems or interesting events
topics for discussion
follow-up lessons

The lessons may be organized according to subject matter, in alphabetical order, by the months, or you may select your own filing device.

LIBRARY. The library, which is also known as the IMC or Instructional Media Center, provides infinite opportunities to teach and learn.

1. Have a contest to guess the number of books in the library. Give the child who comes closest a book of his own.

2. Guess the number of pages in a given book. Again reward the student who comes closest.

3. Make a puzzle game using 3" x 5" cards. Cut the cards into puzzle pieces. Put one piece into a book and write a clue on the other half. Have the students locate the book by using the clues.

4. Compile a list of a variety of resource materials available in the library. Make up a set of questions for the students. Have the students locate the proper book in which to look for an answer to the given question.

5. Have your students make a bulletin board display for the library.

6. When your students have done several book projects, set up a display in the library. (See BOOKS.)

7. Work with the librarian to find books for units of your instruction. Suggest needed books.

8. Teach the students the use of the Dewey Decimal System.

9. Have the students assist the librarian in checking out books and also in reshelving them.

10. Have each student make bookmarkers for the library. They can be made of felt or cloth.

LIMERICKS.   Limericks provide a good opportunity for your students to write creatively.

A limerick is a five-line poem: lines 1, 2, and 5 rhyme; lines 3 and 4 (which are shorter) rhyme.

An example of an original limerick is:

> There once was a man from Kazoo
> Who was floating inside a canoe.
> The canoe was so large
> 'Twas as big as a barge.
> So he sailed it to Kalamazoo.

You may also leave blank spaces in the lines and have the students fill in the blanks. Most poetry books contain some of Lear's limericks. The poetry of Ogden Nash is another source of funny limericks.

Blank limerick:

There once was a bear from the——————— (zoo, shoe)
Whose colors were red, white, and ——————.(blue, ecru)
    The bear's name was Kent
    And he lived in a ————.(tent, vent)
He said "Hello" to Mary and ————.(Sue, you, Drew)

(See POETRY.)

LISTENING.

"Did you hear?"

"No, I wasn't listening."

The art of listening is indeed that. It must be taught just as other subjects must be taught.

Here are some activities that can help to teach the proper listening skills:

1. Gossip. This game requires careful listening. Have the students sit in a circle. Whisper a sentence or story or poem to one of the students. Pass the story along until the last student repeats the story aloud.

One good piece of gossip is this: "The rain in Spain falls mainly in the plain, but the planes in Spain fall mainly in the rain." Use other tongue twisters for the activity.

2. Math Directions. Read several mathematics facts to the students. Allow no pencil or paper. Have the students figure the problems in their head.

Example: Four times seven plus three minus two plus six equals 35.

3. Tape record a lesson on a cassette. Put background noises from a record on the tape. Have the children listen to the tape and listen for the directions. Have them try to block out the background noises.

4. Obtain a record of recorded miscellaneous sounds. They are available from most record stores. Play the record. Have the students guess the sounds. You may do a similar project by using a tape recorder. Record sounds at home, school, or in the city.

5. Have the students close their eyes, close their mouths, and listen to the sounds. Do the same activity inside and outside the classroom.

6. Describe the different types of music and how the students listen differently to each type.

7. Compare the attentiveness of the students when they are listening to rock and roll music, television news programs, cartoons, radio.

8. Have the students memorize a poem, tape record it, and play it back for the class.

9. Have the students list all the sounds they hear in one day. Put them into categories.

10. Have a speaker come to your class. As a lesson, discuss the importance of paying attention to a speaker. Observe your students.

LISTENING CENTERS. Listening centers include a series of head sets (earphones) connected to a tape recorder or record player.

Have the students use the listening center for both learning and pleasure. Vary the type of material so that on at least one day the listening center will contain material of the student's choice.

Establish a listening corner in the room. The components of this corner may include carpets, carpet squares, pillows, hassocks, an electrical outlet, headsets, and record player or recorder.

Tape record reading lessons or have your students tape them for the use of other students. (See TAPE RECORDER.)

— is for the Roman numeral for 1,000; for monumental, which some tasks appear to be; and for miles to go before the education process succeeds.

MACHINES. The study of machines can be done at all levels of instruction, but the intensity of the unit will vary.

The six basic machines are the lever, wheel and axle, the pulley, the inclined plane, the wedge, and the screw.

1. Have the students bring in an assortment of toys and games. Analyze the toys to determine how many simple machines are included. Keep a chart of your findings.

2. Bring in some nails, screws, pieces of metal, wire, used gears. Have the students build a "Machine of the Future." Write a story about their creations.

3. Find other meanings for the words used in the unit. Locate special expressions or phrases.

> Example: "big wheel"—an important person.
> "safety valve"—a play in football.
> "inclination"—a desire to achieve something.

4. Write a letter to a computer company or a car manufacturer to find out more about the advancements in machines.

5. Make a list of all the modern conveniences and machines that were unavailable 50, 100, or 200 years ago. How many are absolutely necessary to survive? Make a chart to compare the jobs of machines today and how the jobs were accomplished 200 years ago.

6. Re-enact the discovery of the wheel. Have the students dress in caveman clothing. Use sign language and facial expressions to create the scene.

7. Set up a small factory in your classroom. Some simple projects include making stuffed pillows, bookmarkers, or potholders. Select a project and have the students assist in the organization and running of the "factory." Use mass production techniques. Analyze the problems and their solutions.

8. Compare farming methods of today to methods of the past. Illustrate some primitive plows and other simple tools.

9. Make a robot with boxes and tinfoil. Have the students name the robot and make him an integral part of the class. The robot may also be a part of an interest center. A student may go inside the robot and answer mathematical questions posed by other members of the class.

10. Make an art design using wheels of various sizes.

11. Make a wheel-mobile. Cut out various sizes of wheels and suspend them from a light in the classroom.

12. Write reports and/or make projects about the following people and their famous inventions:

Alexander Graham Bell	telephone
John Deere	farm machinery
Thomas Alva Edison	lightbulb, etc.
Benjamin Franklin	Franklin stove, etc.
Richard Gatling	Gatling gun
Eli Whitney	cotton gin
Wright Brothers	airplane

MAGAZINES. Keep magazines in your classroom for the following purposes and activities:

1. Make collages with the pictures. An entire bulletin board may be covered with illustrations of people, places, or things obtained from magazines.

2. Cut out the letters from the advertisements and make up your own posters or charts.

3. Take a picture from a magazine. Cover all but a one-inch square. Have the students guess the identity of the picture.

4. Use the magazine to teach reading:

   a. Use the table of contents.

   b. Locate the publisher.

   c. Calculate the cost of the magazine for a year at the single issue price and at the yearly price.

   d. Compare the advertisements in magazines to those which appear in other media.

   e. Select an article and summarize it in a page or less.

   f. Locate various parts of speech in the publication.

   g. Categorize the articles.

   h. Make a generalization about the magazine's readership.

   i. Write a letter to the publisher to obtain information about the cost of production and also the cost for advertisements.

5. Keep a file collection of important articles or useful pictures.

6. Make a list of the magazines available at the public library and also at the school's instructional media center.

7. Make a large magazine of your own. Use oak tag to create your own magazine.

8. Don't cut up the magazines until they have been read.

MAGIC BOX.   A magic box is also known as a black box or a mystery box.

The magic box consists of a box with a mystery object inside it. The object in the magic box will vary according to your purposes.

The students' task is to guess the contents of the box by using their observational skills. A game of twenty questions may also be developed to unlock the mystery of the box. The students may ask questions which may only be answered by *yes* or *no*. A prize may be given to the person who guesses the object's identity.

Put in articles that relate to your instruction. Some possible objects include:

Unit of Study	*Objects*
Language Arts	Piece of newspaper, letters, books, question mark, chalk, eraser, pen.
Science	Arrowheads, pictures of animals, plastic snakes, flowers, wheels, thermometer, test tube, compass.
Social Studies	Stamps, coins, quill pen, eyeglasses, maps, horseshoe, mortar, pestle.
Mathematics	Sphere, word problems, triangle, ruler, cube, recipes, times tables.
Art	Brushes, pictures of famous artists, crayons, styrofoam, scissors, glue.

At the primary level of instruction, the objects should be familiar to the students. The students may also bring in the objects for the magic box. Set up an interest center and have the students make educated guesses about the magic box.

MAGIC CIRCLE. The magic circle is an idea in human relationships. The magic part of the magic circle is the fact that many magical and wonderful outcomes may be the result. The circle part is obvious. Students and teachers move their chairs into a circle to discuss various problems. They may also sit on the floor to hold the magic circle.

The purpose of the magic circle is to have the students and teachers share a "rap session." The teachers and students may develop the rules for the circle together.

Uses for the magic circle:

1. Solve problems with the students by having everyone contribute to the discussion.
2. Develop topics to be covered during a specific unit of instruction.

3. Develop a cooperative feeling among the people in the class by showing each person that you care about him as an individual and also care about his thoughts.
4. The magic circle works well in developing an informal atmosphere for the discussion of drug education topics.
5. The magic circle can become a forum that allows students to air problems with the school or at home. Imaginary situations may also be proposed in which the students think about possible alternatives for solving a problem.
6. Develop a series of attitudes and values through mutual discussions.
7. Change the stereotypes that students have about teachers.
8. Invite the principal to participate in a magic circle. The students will find out that they and the principal have ideas in common.

MAGIC SQUARE. A magic square is a special mathematical figure that contains numbers whose sums of rows, columns, and diagonals equal the same number. (See Figure 9.)

A

8	1	6
3	5	7
4	9	2

B

16	2	3	13
5	11	10	8
9	7	6	12
4	14	15	1

FIGURE 9: **Magic Squares**

Square A totals 15—across, down, and diagonally.
Square B totals 34—across, down, and diagonally.

Magic squares may be used in the following ways:

1. Have the students make up their own magic squares by using one of the basic ones above. This may be accomplished by adding the same number to each part of the square. If you added 2 to each part of Square A, the total would change from 15 to 21.

2. Multiply each number in a magic square and you will create new magic squares. If you multiplied the numbers of Square A by 5, the sum of the columns, rows, and diagonals would be 75.

3. Subtract or add fractions to the numbers.

4. Leave several blank spaces in a square. Tell the students the sum of the square. Have them fill in the blanks.

5. Take tiles (ceramic) and write numbers on them with markers. Make magic squares for each student in this way.

6. Have the students move the rows and columns around to create new magic squares. How many ways can you change one magic square? (An infinite number.)

MAPS.

At the primary level, map instruction must be simple and based on the experiences of the students.

Have the students draw a map of the neighborhood.

Take the students on a mini-field trip around the school. Make a map of the area.

Have the students draw a map from their homes to the school.

Maps may also be used to help the students follow directions. Duplicate a map like the one in Figure 10 and make up a set of directions.

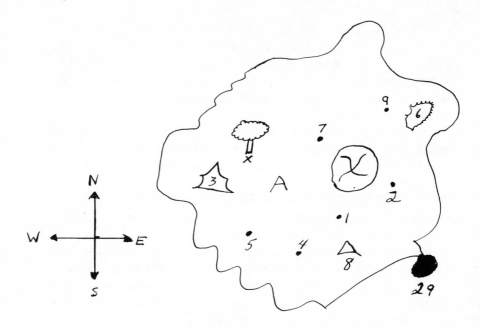

FIGURE 10: **Treasure Map**

FIND THE TREASURE!

1. Read all the directions before beginning. Use a crayon.
2. Join 1 to 4.
3. Join 5 to 2.
4. Put an X on 29.
5. Circle 3.
6. Join 7 to 9.
7. Put a T on the tree.
8. Put a circle around the tree.
9. Do only number 8.
10. Did you follow directions?

130

Activities for Map Instruction:

1. Post the directions—N S E W—in the four corners of your classroom. This will give the students an orientation to directions.

2. Post this sign: "There's NEWS in the wind." Discuss the meaning of this and relate to a weather vane.

3. Make a compass. Use a magnetized needle. You can make one by stroking a needle with a magnet. Suspend the needle above a cork in a container of water. The needle will align itself on a north-south basis.

4. Make a chart showing the intermediate directions— NE, NNW, etc.

5. Relate the word "latitude" to horizontal and lateral. Relate the word "longitude" to long line or vertical.

6. Compare latitude and longitude to streets and roads.

7. Make a map of your classroom, using longitude and latitude as rows across and rows down.

8. Play the "Location Game." Place a series of longitudes and latitudes on the board. Have the students identify the places on a map. Have the students make up their own locations.

Longitude	Latitude	Where am I?
135° E.	20° S.	Australia
0 °	80° W.	Ecuador
90° W.	40° N.	United States (Illinois)
0 °	0°	Atlantic Ocean
150° W.	60° N.	Alaska

9. Panel discussion: How did Columbus plan to reach the East by sailing west?

10. Select ten major cities of the United States. Which ones are located on a river? Why?

11. Play the record "Around the World in 80 Days." Discuss how long it would take to walk around the world. Write a letter to an airline company to find out the speeds of various types of planes.

12. Make a salt, flour, and water map of the United States or of your state. Allow the project to dry and paint with tempera.

Vocabulary Development:

Have the students define and illustrate these and similar terms:

altitude	elevation	north
bay	equator	ocean
boundary line	grid	plateau
canal	gulf	province
cape	hemisphere	river
capital	island	sea
coast	lake	south
continent	latitude	state
delta	longitude	tributary
east	mountains	west

Road Maps:

1. Cut out parts of a road map in the shape of a person.
2. Trace a route from your city to another state.
3. Locate an interstate highway. Trace the route of the even-numbered ones (E-W) and the odd-numbered ones (N-S).
4. Locate state capitals on a map. How are they indicated?
5. Obtain a set of road maps from a local gas station and do an in-depth study of your state.
6. Compare the size of the letters of towns with their populations.
7. Use the scale of miles to measure distances on the map.

8. Locate names of cities in your state that have colors in them. Example. Red Bank, NJ; Greenville, NC; Green Bay, WI.

9. Trace the route of a railroad to determine its beginning and end.

10. Take a road map. Mount it on a sheet of oak tag. Cut the map into puzzle pieces. Put the pieces in a box or an envelope. Set this up as an interest center.

11. Locate airports on a map. Design a new symbol for airports.

12. Make new symbols for the following:

churches	rivers
golf course	county lines
bridges	capitals of states

13. Cut out a small section of a map with no state name indicated. Have the students guess the identity of the state.

14. Look up "maps" and also "cartography" in the encyclopedia.

15. Make a list of other types of maps that are used.

16. Devise a way to fold road maps without problems. Send the method to gasoline companies to see if your directions could be included in future maps.

17. Make a list of the different colors used on a road map.

MATHEMATICS. The teaching of mathematics in the elementary school provides many opportunities for enrichment of the students.

Historical Activities:

1. Have the students describe the measurement devices used in the caveman's time of life. Illustrate the report.

2. Do a research project about the mathematical developments of the Greeks, the Romans, and the Babylonians.

3. Have the students make an abacus. Look up the history of the abacus. Take a vote to see which is faster— a computer or an abacus. (In a recent contest, one man who was extremely

proficient with an abacus solved problems faster than a computer.)

4. Have the students make an oral report about a famous mathematician. Some good possibilities include Copernicus, John Napier, Galileo, and Sir Isaac Newton. People earlier in history include Euclid, Pythagoras, Thales, Archimedes, and Ptolemy.

5. Compare the Roman system of numeration with the Egyptian number system.

6. Have the students find different types of measurements that have changed in history. *Examples:* feet, yards, cubits, rods, peck, and quarts.

6. Compare the knowledge of the students of today with that of students of 500 years ago. Have the students write different concepts that were unknown in the earlier time.

7. Find out the contributions of the Arabic countries to the development of our present numerical system.

8. Hold a round-table discussion on the topic "What would have happened if man had not discovered mathematics?"

Geometry Activities:

1. Have a geometric word play:

> angle—Could it be an angel?
> rectangle—A "wrecked angle."
> circle—"Going around in circles."
> line—Change to "lion."
> geometry—"Gee, I'm a tree!"

2. List all the square, circular, and rectangular objects in the classroom.

3. Count the number of tiles or cement blocks in the classroom. Find out the area of the classroom.

4. Have the students make angles with their hands. Have the other students guess the types of angles that are being formed.

5. Identify the geometric shapes on an automobile. Design an auto with only rectangular shapes or only circular shapes.

6. Make a geometric person; all parts of his body must be made with geometric shapes. Call him or her Geometric George/Georgette.

7. Make geometric shapes with oak tag. Have the students decorate them.

8. Obtain a box of sugar cubes. Make a sugar sculpture and then measure the volume of the sculpture.

9. Compare a square inch to a square centimeter. Compare a square foot to a square meter.

10. Cut out various geometric shapes and make them into a puzzle.

11. Make a mosaic with ceramic tiles. Find the area covered by various colors.

12. Make several geometric structures with toothpicks or tongue depressors.

13. Cut several cubes from a piece of wood. Put letters on each one. Make them into geometric words.

14. Have the students design a new geometric shape. Draw it. Give it a new name.

15. Use the clock to determine angles, circles, radius, and diameter.

16. Use geometric shapes to create a man of the future.

17. Make a three-dimensional sculpture. Use rectangular prisms, cylinders, dowels, triangular prisms, or spheres. Nail or glue in place.

18. Construct a geometric mobile and suspend it from the lights.

19. Make a geometric shape into a person. Put large shapes on the students and have them describe the figure.

20. Make and use a geoboard.

Take a ½ inch piece of pine. Insert five rows of nails equally spaced across and down.

Geoboards may also be made of plexiglass. Cut a square of plexiglass that is ¼ inch thick. Drill holes in the required pattern. Put nuts and bolts in the holes. Use this geoboard with the overhead projector.

Use rubber bands or string to give examples of various geometric shapes. The students can each use an individual geoboard to work with area and length of plane figures.

The geoboards may also be used to develop concepts in graphing.

The Basics of Mathematics:

1. Use the calendar as a counting device and also as a multiplication table.

2. Put various problems in each day of the calendar. Have the students solve them. (See CALENDAR.)

3. Cover a hanger with yarn. Use clothespins as counters.

4. Make a set of silent counters. Use oak tag or purchase washers from a hardware store. Poker chips may also be used.

5. Make puzzles out of the homework assignments. Take a worksheet and cut it into puzzle pieces. Have the students write the answers to the puzzle. Cover this worksheet with Con-Tact paper.

6. Make a number line with vinyl. Use plastic tape for the numbers.

7. Use ceramic tiles (1 inch) for making math games. Write both numbers and operations on the tiles with markers. Be sure the markers are permanent.

8. Use styrofoam egg cartons to make an addition table, a multiplication table, or for sorting sets of objects.

9. Bring in money from a foreign country. Compare to our money. (See DOLLAR BILL INQUIRY.)

10. Make a chart showing the basic rules of arithmetic. Post it in a prominent place. Be sure to include *greater than*, *less than*, and *equal to*.

11. Make a chart comparing the speeds of man and of vehicles.

Man walking	4 miles per hour
Man running	15 miles per hour
Cars	60 miles per hour
Airplanes	600 miles per hour
Rockets	25,000 miles per hour

12. Make a display of objects and pictures. Have the students fill in the proper units of measure for:

_____elephants
_____apples
_____cars
_____nails
_____spices

13. Use a foreign language to reinforce basic addition facts. Post an arithmetic chart in another language. Write problems in the other language. Have the students solve the problems.

Example: The numbers one to ten in Swahili are:

1—moja	6—sita
2—mbili	7—saba
3—tatu	8—nane
4—nne	9—tisa
5—tano	10—kumi

moja plus moja equals_____
tano plus tano equals_____

14. The same activity may be done in Spanish.

1—uno	6—seis	11—once
2—dos	7—siete	12—doce
3—tres	8—ocho	13—trece
4—cuatro	9—nueve	14—catorce
5—cinco	10—diez	15—quince

15. Use candy bars to have the students measure length and width. They may also be used for weight.

16. Use playing cards for teaching multiplication facts. Have the students select two cards and multiply them. This may also be done with addition, subtraction, and division.

17. Make a chart of the hours in a week. Keep track of the time spent eating, sleeping, going to school, watching television, and other activities. Calculate these amounts for a year.

18. Fill a box with dried beans. Take five handfuls. Estimate the number of beans. Count them. Compare the results.

19. Use dice to develop a math game. Roll the dice and add or multiply the numbers that appear.

20. Have the students write original math problems. Put them on ditto masters. Run them off for other students.

21. Make up a code with the alphabet and numbers. Make up addition or subtraction problems with the answers equal to letters of the alphabet.

22. Take a survey of the class. Some possible questions to use are:

> What television shows do you watch on Sunday?
> How many eggs do you eat a week?
> What is your favorite subject?

Tabulate the results of the survey.

23. Guess the number of pages in a given book. Compare your estimate to the actual amount.

24. Write word problems with different sports as the theme.

> Football — yards, goals, points, minutes, touchdowns
> Hockey — minutes, goals, penalties, length of game
> Baseball — walks, strikes, innings, hits, runs, errors
> Basketball — penalties, foul shots, goals, quarters
> Tennis — set, match, love, let, sphere, graphs (rackets)
> Track — decathlon, miles, meters, minutes, feet
> Fighting — rounds, time, knockouts, seconds, punches
> Swimming — length, volume, seconds, fractions of seconds

Fractional Activities:

1. Use this mnemonic device: nUmerator—U means up.
   Denominator—D means down.

2. Look up the word *fraction* in the dictionary. Relate this to *fracture*—broken parts.

3. Make a bulletin board entitled "Fractured Fractional Fiction."

4. Make a fraction pie—a real one. Use salt, flour, and water, and bake in a tin pie plate. Make several pies for various fractions.

5. Use money to teach fractions. Use either real money or play money. Some fractional equivalents that can be taught with money are wholes, halves, quarters, fifths, tenths, twentieths, and hundredths.

6. Make a wheel of fractions. Place the numerators on the outside of the wheel. Add a movable inner wheel for the denominators.

7. Use candy to teach fractions. Have the students make sets of candy and then take away half or a fifth. The candy should be covered with paper so that it can be used repeatedly during the lesson.

8. Draw a fraction on a large sheet of paper. Make the fraction into a person or an animal.

9. Make a list of items that have fractions as the basis for their name: octopus—eight; centipede—one hundred; millepede—one thousand; insects—divided into sections; half a pound, etc.

10. Make a fraction box. Whenever a student sees an article or picture using fractions, he should put in into the box.

11. Use the stock market section of the newspaper to compare fractions.

Sources for Mathematical Activities:

1. Use a menu from a restaurant. Have the students figure the cost of a given meal.

2. Use the telephone and the telephone directory for activities. Make up problems using the dial (or push button). Add the values for these letters: G+E+O+M+E+T+R+Y =
$$4+3+6+6+3+8+7+9 = 46$$
Reverse the order and find the words corresponding to the numbers: 4+3+5+5+6 = HELLO

Make a list of the people in the phone book with colors as a part of their name. How many Browns are in the book? Greens?

Which person in the class has the largest sum when you add each letter according to the telephone dial? Use the person's full name.

3. Calorie charts may also be helpful. Make up problems using a calorie chart. This can also be integrated with a health unit.

4. Write a letter to an airline company and obtain an airfare chart telling the cost of various flights. Compare the costs of a first class vs. charter vs. coach vs. night or weekend rates.

5. Use the music scales to teach fractional notes.

6. Use car odometers and speedometers. Keep track of the number of miles traveled and the number of gallons of gasoline used. Calculate the cost of keeping the car for a year. Figure out how many miles per gallon the car gets.

7. Ask a car dealer for a copy of the new car accessory list. Order an imaginary car with certain options and have the students figure the cost.

8. Use a calculator to help supplement your program.

9. Use the bank to help you with checks, interest, services of banks, etc.

METRICS. The metric measurement system will gradually find its way into our lives.

1. Make a bulletin board with the title "DiaMETRICally Opposed." Compare the metric system with the English system of measurement.

2. Make a diagram of your classroom. Use the metric system for all measurements.

3. Study the language of the metric system. Relate the words to the experiences of the students. *Example:* The prefix "centi-" means hundred—century, cent, centenary, centennial, centigrade, per cent; "deci-" means ten—decade, decimal, December (originally was 10th month); "milli-" means thousand—million (thousand thousands), millenial, millepede.

4. Translate road signs into the metric system.

NEW YORK CITY——100 km——(62.137 mi.)

5. Locate quotations, expressions, song titles, or phrases that contain weights, measurements, or distances. Change them to the metric system.

"Walk a mile in my shoes."	_____km.
"Sixteen Tons"	_____kg.
"I can't fathom that."	_____m.
pound for pound	_____kg.
inchworm	_____cm.
gallon of milk	_____l.
square yard of material	_____sq. m.
100-yard dash	_____m.

6. Look up the history of metric measurement. Make a list of the countries that do not use the metric system.

7. Make up your own system of measurement. Compare yours to the metric system.

8. Measure the length and width of a dollar bill in both systems.

9. Make a list of the various changes that would be made if America became 100% metric tomorrow. Include sports, businesses, gasoline stations, recipes, etc.

10. Use sugar cubes to measure volume in metric measurement and in the English system.

11. Have the students estimate the total length of spaghetti served in the school on a given day. Measure string licorice in a package.

12. Have the students go to the blackboard and draw a meter without using any measurement devices. Compare with a metric ruler.

13. Estimate the length of your shoes, the span of your hand, and the circumference of your head. Measure to find the exact figures.

14. Mark off a kilometer outside the school. Have the children walk that distance to see how long it would take. Time the results.

15. Change a recipe from the English system to metrics.

16. Obtain a metric scale (bathroom-type scale). Weigh each person in the class and post a chart of the metric weights.

17. Measure the dimensions of a piece of paper in inches and also in centimeters. Cut a piece of paper to a specific dimension.

18. Make a balance scale or obtain one from the science laboratory. Weigh several objects and make a chart of their measurements.

19. Have a baseball-throwing contest. Measure the throws in metrics.

20. Make a list of all the ways in which numbers are a part of your life. Add to this list throughout the year.

MNEMONIC DEVICES. Mnemonics are tricks or word associations that are used to help improve one's memory.

Mathematics:

"Thirty days hath September. . ."	months of the year
div<u>is</u>ible	"If you're wise, you use your i's."
n<u>U</u>merator, <u>D</u>enominator	U=up, D=down
Friday the 13th	bad luck

Social Studies:

"Columbus sailed the ocean blue in 1492."
"Boston Indians dumped some tea in 1773."
"A signature did Hancock affix in 1776."

Music:

Lines of the staff: E G B D F—"Every Good Boy Does Fine."
                     G B D F A—"Good Boys Do Fine Always."
Spaces of the Staff: F A C E—Spells "Face."
                     A C E G—"All Cows Eat Grass."

Science:

stalaGmite, stalaCtite   G=ground, C=ceiling

Language Arts:

synonym	S=same, N=name.
principal	The princiPAL is your PAL.
stationEry	The "E" stands for the envelope.
desert, deSSert	The "SS" stands for two helpings.
angel	The angEL is ELevated.
all right	All right is like all wrong.
cemetery	You say "EEEEEEEE" in a cemetery.
altogether	It has four words—Al to get her.
handkerchief	It has two words—hand and kerchief.
library	It is not like strawberry or blueberry.

MOBILES: A mobile is literally a very moving experience. Mobiles may be suspended from the lights in the classroom or from specially hung wires.

    1. Use coat hangers to create mobiles. Cover the hangers with yarn or wool. Hang various vocabulary words from the hangers.

    2. Use a styrofoam egg carton to create a mobile. Suspend string from each compartment. Hang pictures of natural scenes from each.

3. Use seashells to create a sea-mobile. Drill holes in the shells. Tie the shells together with fish net or yarn.

4. Suspend a dowel on a string. Attach word cards, geometric shapes, pieces of cloth or chimes to create a mobile.

5. Suspend a large cube and paint or paste pictures on all sides.

Other materials and themes for mobiles:

> Modern decorations.
> Santa Claus and other holidays of the year.
> Synonyms, antonyms, and homonyms.
> Dried flowers and plants.
> Toothpick sculpture.
> Bottle caps.
> Balsa wood creations.
> Bamboo wind chimes that you make yourself.
> Beads.

MOTIVATION. Motivation is a vital part of the teaching and learning process.

Several ways to motivate a lesson about discovery and exploration follow:

Topic: **Discovery and Exploration—Christopher Columbus**

1. Play the record "Sitting on the Dock of the Bay." Discuss how this applies to the discovery of foreign lands.

2. Make a bulletin board with the title, "Columbus Goofed—the World Is Flat!"

3. Play the hangman game with the students.

4. Speak several words in Spanish and have the students guess their meanings. Relate this to Columbus' background.

5. Make up a "change a letter" worksheet. Give clues for each word. Change the word SHIP to DOCK.

> a. SHIP
> b. When you fall on a banana peel   SLIP
> c. When you hit someone   SLAP
> d. Helps to keep you clean   SOAP
> e. What you do in a tub   SOAK

f. It's on your foot   SOCK
g. A place for a ship   DOCK

6. Give the students some spice cookies. Discuss the history of spices.

7. Put a ship or a picture of a ship in a small box. Have the students guess the object in twenty questions.

8. Play the record "Raindrops Keep Falling on My Head." Tell the students that Columbus heard this record while he was on his way to his discoveries. Discuss.

9. Take a volleyball or a red playground ball and deflate it. Throw it on the classroom floor and say, "See. This is just like the world—flat." Discuss this statment.

10. Pose a question to the class: "What would have happened to America if Columbus had not discovered it?"

11. Take a picture of Columbus. Cut it into puzzle pieces. Set this up as a center.

12. Make a word find from the words "Christopher Columbus." *Examples:* bus, coal, crush.

13. Give each child a piece of Genoa salami. Tell them that this has something to do with Columbus. Have them do some research to find the connection.

14. Make a picture of a dock with electric signs, modern buildings, cars, airplanes, and modern conveniences. Tell the students that this is a real picture of what Columbus saw when he discovered America. Have the students make the corrections.

MURALS. Murals may be used to introduce, develop, or culminate a unit of study. A mural is a large painting or illustration with a central theme or idea.

Use kraft paper or poster paper for the mural. Use tempera, water colors, pastels, or crayons for the mural. Spray fixative will help to preserve the mural for future use.

Suggested themes for murals:

From Sea to Shining Sea
America the Beautiful

It's a Small World
The Indians—Our First People
George Crossed the Delaware
Life Cycle of Plants
Pollution
Sports Throughout the Ages
City of the Future
The Olympics
The Story of the Wheel
Our Country—North, South, East, and West
Communication Throughout the Ages

MUSIC. The teaching of music belongs in everyone's classroom. The appreciation of music can last throughout one's life.

1. Music flash cards: Place the names and pictures of various instruments and terms in music on flash cards. Make a contest with two teams competing for the answers.

2. Make up a song for a social studies or science lesson. Use a familiar tune and make up words that fit the tune. The following song could be sung to "Mary Had a Little Lamb."

Volcanoes erupt with lava, erupt with lava, erupt with lava.
Volcanoes erupt with lava, and the ashes fall all around.
The lava flows just like a river, like a river, like a river.
The lava flows just like a river, and moves down to the sea.

This activity helps to develop concepts and also provides a musical experience.

3. Make a list of famous television commercials and theme songs. Record them and have the students identify them. Do the same for movie themes.

4. Have the students bring in records. Write down the lyrics. Determine which are prose and which are poetry. Use this for creative writing as well.

5. Use the various musical notes and rests to create an art project.

6. Have an international music day. Play songs from around the world. Compare these to the music of today in America.

7. Create original musical instruments from junk.

8. In order to obtain your students' attention, sing to them.

9. Use the tape recorder and have the students sing songs.

10. Make up a set of questions whose answers may be found in the words of songs.

Where did you meet your wife?—"On Top of Old Smokey."
What is your name?—"Clementine."
Who runs your farm?—"Old MacDonald."

11. Make a matching exercise using musical terms and expressions. Mix up the answers. The students may also make up some.

A. A kind of ball	—bass (base)
B. A pointed scissors is	—sharp
C. Part of a fish	—scale
D. Used by a shepherd	—staff
E. What you do at night	—rest
F. Part of a dollar	—quarter, half, whole
G. Having to do with nature	—natural
H. What a reporter writes	—notes
I. ___as a pancake	—flat
J. A dumb bell is a __bell	—bar
K. The last part of a letter	—signature
L. Used to open a door	—key
M. Use a ruler to__	—measure
N. An Army officer	—major
O. Not a major but a __	—minor
P. A policeman walks a__	—beat
Q. A prison	—Sing Sing
R. A billboard	—sign
S. A piece of stone	—rock
T. Put a hot dog in a__	—roll
U. Reds, whites, and__	—blues

147

V. Used to make bread   —do (dough)
W. Four people giving haircuts   —barbershop quartet
X. A geometric dance   —square dance
Y. The third month   —March
Z. Circular; part of a boxing match   —round

— stands for a grade that means needs improvement; for the needs of students, which must be met; and for novelty, which is needed to maintain student interest.

NEWSPAPERS. The use of newspapers in the classroom is effective. Newspapers may be used in all areas of the curriculum.

The newspaper may be used on a daily basis for a short period of time, on a weekly basis, or as a unit of instruction for several weeks. It may be used as the entire curriculum for a day—using no reading materials other than the newspaper.

Language Arts:

1. Use the index of the newspaper to locate the various departments in the paper.

2. Keep track of the headlines. List the nouns and verbs that appear for a week.

3. Make a list of some possible uses for old newspaper.

4. Make a bulletin board that shows the history of communication throughout the ages.

5. Read three articles and write the main idea from each one.

6. Make a vocabulary list of parts of the newspaper. Make a newspaper dictionary.

7. Make a list of the bylines of a day's paper. Determine which people are local and which are national.

8. Devise an award system to recognize the outstanding article or news coverage for the week.

9. Make a collection of different types of leads—summary, question, statement, or description.

10. Make a list of special abbreviations found in the paper.

11. Make a list of action words that appear in the sports section. List helping verbs and compound verbs.

12. Read an article and find synonyms for difficult words.

13. Study unusual words in the headlines. Look them up in the dictionary. Re-write the headlines, using your own words.

14. Find compound words in the paper.

15. Find words ending in -s, -ed, and -ing.

16. Re-write the headlines to make them into complete sentences.

17. Search through the paper to locate spelling or grammar mistakes.

18. Compare the various sizes of type and styles of printing. Create a box with different styles of printing. Make this into an interest center.

19. Take a picture from the newspaper. Mount it and describe it in 25 words or less.

20. Locate a picture of a man, a woman, and a child. Make them into an imaginary family and describe them in a story.

21. Make a list of the different types of automobiles sold through the newspaper. Put them in alphabetical order.

22. Make a list of all the various advertisements in the ad section. Write an original ad to sell something in the classroom.

23. In the food advertisements, make a list of all the produce items, meat items, or dairy items listed.

24. Select a page of a newspaper. List the numbers of periods, commas, question marks, and exclamation marks. Compare them.

25. Cut the headlines out of the newspaper. Put the article on the board. Have the students write an original headline.

26. Find ten words that contain a silent letter.

27. Select ten words that you think would stump other students. Define these words. Find another person and give him the definitions. Have him guess the word.

28. Establish your own newspaper. Organize the newspaper on the basis of a local one. Have various reporters to cover the different sections. Serve as advisor to the paper.

29. Read a comic. Draw your own and write in the bubbles.

30. Find an article that will answer the questions: who, what, when, where, and why? Answer the questions.

31. Write a story based on an advertisement. What happened before the advertisement? What happened after it?

32. Select a picture from the paper. Have the students write an original story about the picture.

33. Make a list of the adjectives that describe the nouns on the first page of the paper.

34. Compare the news articles in two different newspapers. What are the differences in writing style and vocabulary?

35. Have the students cut up the newspaper and create a mixed-up story.

Social Studies:

1. Locate the places mentioned on page one on a map.

2. Categorize the stories into local, county, state, national, and international.

3. Make a list of the different factories mentioned in the paper. Write letters to them to learn more about their products.

4. Make a list of the various types of transportation mentioned in the paper. Do a report about one of them.

5. List all the cities, states, and countries mentioned in the paper. Alphabetize them.

6. Cut out the names of various cities. Write letters to each to obtain more information about them.

7. Clip out pictures of famous people. Make them into a "Who's Who" bulletin board. Have the students match the pictures with the articles.

8. Locate different climates in the paper. Compare the ways the people live and dress.

9. Make a list of ten different occupations mentioned in the paper. Discuss the qualifications of the various careers.

10. Make a list of the various articles dealing with politics and government. Which officials were elected? Which ones are appointed?

11. Look at the home advertisements. Compare the prices for different houses.

12. Follow an event for a week to determine the course the article follows.

Science:

1. Predict the weather for a week. Compare your predictions to the real thing.

2. Change the weather forecasts and events into metric measurement.

3. Try to find articles that tell about new inventions or discoveries in science. Make a bulletin board displaying these articles.

4. Look up the history of printing. Have the students write a report on the various types of printing and the new processes used to print newspapers.

5. Recycle newspaper. Shred the paper into small pieces and mix with water in a large bucket. Mix with blender, adding lint from dryer. Filter out the water with a screen. Press with an iron. Allow the paper to dry.

6. Find the highs and lows in the weather. Make a list of the specialized vocabulary used in weather reporting, such as *front, high, low,* and *hurricane.*

7. Follow the articles dealing with gardening and plants. Make a collection of hints to home gardeners.

8. Make a pollution bulletin board containing articles and pictures about ecology, nature, and the effects of pollution. Write letters to factories to find out what they are doing to help solve their pollution problems.

9. Find the health column in the paper. Write your own health advice column.

10. Find an article about space and space exploration. Look up the history of space travel in the encyclopedia. Make an interest center dealing with space.

11. Find a story about the future. Draw a person of the future.

12. Make a list of problems facing farmers today. Compare to the problems of farmers two hundred years ago.

13. Locate an article about an accident. Design a modern car that will prevent accidents.

14. Find five articles about animals. Draw a picture of each animal. Write a report about one.

15. Locate articles dealing with endangered animals. Write a letter to an animal preservation organization.

16. Find an article dealing with an operation. Write an original play dealing with the hospital.

17. Make a list of the various types of fabrics mentioned in advertisements. Find out how each is made. Categorize them also as natural, man-made, or synthetic.

18. How many different appliances mentioned in the paper run on electricity? Write a letter to the local electric company to find out more about its operations.

19. How many people were admitted to or released from the hospital in today's paper? Write a story about the time you went to a doctor.

20. Find an article about a machine. Draw it. Write a story about the machine.

Mathematics:

1. Find out the cost of an advertisement in the newspaper. Compare the cost of a full page ad to a half page, a quarter page, and an advertisement on the front page.

2. Use the want ads to locate a car that costs less than $500.

3. Have the students write original articles based on the advertisement section of the newspaper.

4. Use the television guide of the paper to plan a week's worth of television watching.

5. Measure the headlines of each page. Measure the size of the articles on various pages. Find out how the newspaper measures articles.

6. Compare the length of local and international articles. Which ones are longer? Why?

7. Have the students locate an advertised car that is similar to your car.

8. Keep track of the number of pages in the newspaper for a week. Which day has the largest paper? Why? Compare the number of advertisements in the paper for each day of the week.

9. Make a list of ten different numbers used in the paper. Write a sentence for each one.

10. Plan a vacation to a place mentioned in the newspaper. Write a letter to a local travel agent for information. Have the students plan an itinerary.

11. Use the stock market pages to add and subtract fractions. Buy an imaginary or real stock and trace its progress for a month. Have the students calculate their imaginary losses or gains.

12. Use the food advertisements to have the students plan a meal. Allow them $50.00 worth of groceries. Have them make a list of their purchases.

13. Use the food ads to develop comparison shopping. Discuss the use of coupons. How much money is actually saved?

14. Compare the quantities of articles advertised. Which item is cheaper—a ten-pack of soda for $1.49 or a half-gallon for 97¢? Write similar problems, using prices in the paper.

15. Use the sports section to write various problems dealing with scores from previous games. Have the students calculate wins and losses for the year.

16. How many shares of a certain stock can you purchase for $1,000? See which day of the week is the best one on which to buy the stock.

17. Have the students "purchase" a house from the paper. In which section of the newspaper will you find houses for sale? In which section of the city will the students purchase the home? Why?

18. Locate the service section in the paper. Compare their costs with the costs you would find if you did the job yourself.

19. Compare the costs of traveling to the next city by bus, air, train, or car. Which is the most convenient? Which is the least expensive?

20. Use the obituary section to find out how many people died yesterday. What was the average age? How many were men? How many were women? How many people were under age 20?

21. Find the average cost of renting a house or an apartment. How many do not allow children? How many do not allow pets?

22. Use the food section to list the five most expensive items advertised. Find the five least expensive items. How many items are less than 25¢?

Art:

1. Using the paper, make a collage.
2. Make paper airplanes and try to fly them.
3. Make a series of paper dolls or a paper tree.
4. Cut out a picture and decorate it with a moustache, or paint around it.

5. Use the newspaper to make a papier mache animal.
6. Use the newspaper to stuff pillows or stuffed animals.
7. Make a list of all the art exhibits in the area.

— stands for zero, for open-minded people, and for obstacles which can be surmounted.

OBJECTIVES.   Behavioral objectives are the basic tools that help the teacher and the students to develop.

To be effective, behavioral objectives should be clear and concise, should be measurable in observable behavior, should contain a standard of achievement, and should set levels of acceptance.

Uses of Objectives:

Place behavioral objectives on learning stations so that the child can read them and measure his progress toward the achievement of the prescribed goal.

Write behavioral objectives for each student in a learning contract. Gear the objective to meet the child's specific learning style and academic needs.

Organize the units of instruction based on the behavioral objectives.

In the process of evaluation, the behavioral objectives you write will establish the basis for determining student achievement.

Samples of Objectives:

1. As a result of the lesson, the child will be able to add a series of two-digit numbers, with carrying, at a competence level of 80%.

2. The students will silently read pages 42 through 47, will be able to list three main characters of the selection, and will write a sentence about each character.
3. The students will write a personal letter and will be able to list all the following parts: heading, greeting, body, closing, and signature.

Behavioral objectives should include words like do, read, recite, list, calculate, perform, etc.

OPEN HOUSE. "The Open House" is frequently a time of learning for both the parents and the teacher. It usually occurs during an evening meeting of the home and school association.

Suggestions for a successful "Open House" night:

1. Be yourself.
2. Pre-plan and know exactly what you will say to the parents. You might practice earlier in the evening if it helps you.
3. Tell the parents the expectations you have for the up-coming year.
4. Tell the parents your standards of homework, neatness, and behavior.
5. Discuss the curriculum for your grade level. Detail some special projects for the year.
6. Give general recommendations as to how parents can help the child at home.
7. Take the parents through a series of mini-lessons to give them an idea of the day's activities.
8. Avoid personal conferences at this time. If a parent wishes a conference, set up a conference at a later date.

OPEN SPACE. Open space schools are those that have eliminated many of the walls—both physical and psychological—of education. Many modern approaches to learning and teaching take place in an open space environment.

However, the open space concept of education can and does take place in self-contained situations.

Here are a few general ways to open your classroom (self-contained or otherwise):

1. Use learning stations and interest centers. (See INTEREST CENTERS.)

2. Make an effort to individualize your method of instruction. (See INDIVIDUALIZATION.)

3. Obtain a rug and establish a quiet reading center—a place where the students can lie on the floor and learn.

4. Have the students actively participate in the learning process by suggesting activities for given units of instruction.

5. Move your desk to the back of the room.

6. Allow the students to sit in groups of their choice.

7. Use the doors and walls for learning areas.

8. Find different ways to present the material—putting on plays, giving oral reports, making tape recordings, using audio-visual aids, and using speakers.

9. Visit an open space school to observe different or novel methods of instruction.

10. Evaluate your teaching, and as you feel a need to change, change. You are the most important factor in teaching and in developing your idea of the open space concept.

ORGANIZATION.

Tips for organizing your class and materials:

1. Use egg cartons for storing paper clips, fasteners, tacks, or small objects.

2. Use ditto master boxes covered with Con-Tact paper to store homework assignments.

3. Make an in-class library. Use pay envelopes from the bank to make pockets for the cards.

4. Number and label your records and tapes. Make a cross-reference file according to the subjects.

5. Create a creative writing file and a picture file. (See LESSON PLANS and DO IT YOURSELF.)

OUTLINING. Outlining skills are vitally needed at the elementary level and all higher levels of instruction.
Have the students categorize objects in a set:

television, radio, movies ____communication media
apples, tomatoes, pears ____fruits
Monitor, Mayflower, Pinta ____historical ships

Vary the format of this exercise by having the students list items that would be under a main category:

cities ____New York, Philadelphia, Los Angeles
Presidents of the U.S. ___Truman, Lincoln, Washington
sports ____golf, tennis, football, baseball

After the students have developed the concepts of main ideas or main topics and sub-topics, have them work on a basic outline:

United States History

1. Colonial Patriots
   A. George Washington
      1._____
      2._____
      3._____
   B. Thomas Jefferson
      1._____
      2._____
      3._____

Have the students use a topic outline at first and then develop it into a sentence outline. They must know the basic format of an outline and its purpose in order to eventually make their own outlines.
Change this outline into a sentence outline (the topic is imaginary):

The Fuzzy, Dizzy-Nosed Cat

I. Appearance
  A. Size
  B. Shape
  C. Coloration
II. Habits
  A. Eating
  B. Visitations
III. Friends
  A. Red dogs
  B. Yellow deer
  C. Blue jays

As the students develop their outlining skills, additional details and topics may be added.

Have the students copy an outline from the board to practice the format.

Mix up an outline and have the students put it in the correct sequence.

Outline a page from the social studies or science book. Have the students read it and see if your outline is correct.

After the students have developed an outline, have them write an oral report based on it.

Make a sequential outline.

Have the students outline a "How To." A "How To" tells someone the way to accomplish something. Some "How To's" are:

1. Bake a cake.
2. Write a letter.
3. Make a peanut butter sandwich.
4. Do a dance.
5. Sharpen a pencil.
6. Sew a dress.
7. Make a meatball and spaghetti dinner.
8. Tie your shoes.

OVERHEAD PROJECTOR. The overhead projector is used to project transparencies.

1. Instead of using the chalkboard, use the overhead to write mathematical problems, write sentences, and correct errors.

2. The overhead will project opaque objects as a dark outline. Have the students identify these objects.

3. Use the overhead projector to create shadow figures with your hands.

4. Colorful creations may be made by mixing food coloring and water in a container and projecting the container onto the screen.

5. Live insects may be projected with the overhead.

6. Magnetic lines of force will be displayed if they are projected. Put iron filings between two sheets of plastic or glass and move a magnet over them. (See TRANSPARENCIES.)

— stands for pupils, for personalization, and for progress in the learning process.

PENMANSHIP. The art of good penmanship has become a lost art, but it can be revived in your classroom.

After the students have mastered the basic letter formation procedures—the proper letter formations, neatness, proper posture, holding of the writing instrument, etc. — enrichment and reinforcement activities are needed.

1. Obtain a copy of the Declaration of Independence or the Constitution of the United States. Have the students copy the different letter formations. Write your own "Declaration of Writing Independence." This would be done on a large chart and would include all of the students' penmanship.

2. Make a writing bulletin board. On mural paper, have each student write with a felt marker. Encourage neatness and proper letter formation.

3. Have the students practice writing on the chalkboard. Have them write with their right hands, their left hands, and also write blindfolded. Compare the differences.

4. Have the students write a paragraph of their choice. Put this in a folder and compare it with various samples throughout the year.

5. Make a bulletin board with the title of "PEN MAN SHIP Through the Ages." Place various types of writing on the board.

6. Obtain a copy of a book from colonial days. Compare colonial penmanship to today's type of writing and typing.

7. Have the students write with various writing instruments — felt tip pens, pencils, pens, crayons, chalk, and pastels — to create differences in texture.

8. Make a display of writing instruments from the Stone Age to the Space Age.

9. Write letters to other schools in other states in order to obtain pen pals.

10. Have the students develop a method of writing for the future. Find a symbol for each letter of the alphabet.

11. Do a research project about different forms of writing — cuneiform, Phoenician, Chinese, Greek, Hebrew, and Roman.

12. Make a penmanship center. Give an award to the person with the best penmanship each week.

13. Write an assignment on a ditto or on the board so that none of the students can read it. Use this as an example of poor penmanship. Hold a discussion to obtain the students' reaction.

PHOTOGRAPHY.   Photography can be taught to elementary school students. The students may take pictures to supplement class projects and improve class instruction.

Instamatic cameras are relatively inexpensive. Black and white film will help to reduce costs. Many processing labs offer specials in newspapers and magazines.

1. Take photos of each child and make a class photo album. Have the students write captions for the pictures.
2. Use photos to supplement oral and written reports.
3. Record important events during the week.
4. Photograph the school and make an ecological survey.
5. Take "before" and "after" pictures of projects.
6. Take sequential pictures and write a narration for them.

Your local photography store will frequently offer assistance in selecting materials and in processing. The high school's photography department may also offer help.

Invite a professional photographer to speak to your students. (See CAMERA.)

PHYSICAL EDUCATION. The physical education program at the elementary level frequently involves the utilization of the physical education specialist. Some schools, however, do not have this specialist.

Without this help, what can an elementary teacher do?

1. Establish a set of objectives for your students or obtain a copy of the school's physical education curriculum.

2. List the activities for your students in relationship to the listed objectives.

3. Individualize the instruction by having students participate in activities at their own developmental level.

4. As a pre-physical education activity, have the students develop a project about one of these sports and activities:

angling	golf	softball
archery	gymnastics	speedball
badminton	handball	swimming
basketball	hockey	table tennis
bowling	horsemanship	tennis
dance	lacrosse	track and field
fencing	skiing	volleyball
football	skin diving	weightlifting
field hockey	soccer	wrestling

5. During the physical education period, play an organized game with the students. This will have a positive influence on the game and also upon the students' attitudes.

6. Teach the rules of the games before they are played. Be sure all the students understand the basics.

7. Mix teams in group activities so that the good athletes and those not quite as capable can compete.

8. Have the students serve as referees or umpires during the games.

9. Use mistakes of the students to develop an acceptance of others' mistakes. This will also help to develop good sportsmanship.

10. Rotate the role of leader or captain so that all the students can lead the class.

11. Begin each physical education period with a series of exercises — running in place, arm twists, push-ups, or sit-ups.

PLANTS.   The study of plant life usually occurs at all levels in the learning process. The spring is usually the best time for this unit. It may also be taught in connection with a unit on animals.

One approach to a unit is to develop problems and suggest ways to solve them.

Problem: Why do plants need sunlight?

1. Make a bulletin board with the title, "Our Sun—Who Needs It?"
2. Write a story about "The Day the Sun Didn't Shine."
3. Grow two plants. Water them the same. Place one in the sun and the other where it receives no light.
4. Do a research project on solar energy.
5. Write a letter to the local electric or gas utility for information.

Problem: How do plants grow?

1. Grow seeds in three different ways — without soil, without water, and without light. Observe the results.
2. Add special plant food to some plants and none to others.
3. Talk to your plants. Set up a control experiment so that you talk nicely to one set of plants, ignore others, and sing to others. You may also talk unkindly to a set of plants. Observe the results in growth.
4. Perform an experiment with celery and colored water. Place the celery in a jar of water and add food color-

ing. Observe the colored water traveling through the veins.

5. Start several seedlings in milk cartons. Cover them with blue, green, yellow, red, violet, and transparent cellophane. Cover one with an opaque material. Observe the results.

Problem: How do plants make food?

1. Have the students develop a play. The various parts are played by the roots, stems, sun, chlorophyll, soil, and minerals. Have each student portray his part.
2. Make a filmstrip showing the life cycle of a plant. (See FILMSTRIPS.)
3. Bring in a cross section of a tree and have the students observe the growth rings.
4. Obtain a piece of sugar cane. Cut it and give samples to the students.

Problem: What are the uses for plants?

1. Make a chart with the following:

Parts of the Plant	Example
roots	
stem	
bark	
flowers	
fruits	
leaf	

Have the students fill in the examples.

2. Draw a large plant on the bulletin board. Put pictures from magazines on the various parts of the plant.

General Activities for the Unit:

1. Have the students define the following:

plants	leaves	chlorophyll
seeds	mushrooms	trees
evergreen	deciduous	pollen

2. Have each child make a collection of plants found on a field trip in the school area.

POETRY.   The study of poetry can be exciting. Your attitude toward the teaching of poetry will be evident to the students.

A first step in poetry teaching is to read poems to the students and have them read poems to you.

Poetry may be integrated with other subjects. Make an outline map of a state or country. Have the students write a poem in the outline.

Shape Poems:

Poems may be all sizes and shapes. One example is the square poem, written on the sides of a square or rectangle. (See Figure 11.)

America is a place that's great

Here's what he has to say:

HELLO, AMERICA.

People visit us each day

Our President is the head of State

FIGURE 11:   **Square Poem**

Another example of a shape poem is a triangular one (Figure 12). You may read the poem from any side of the triangle.

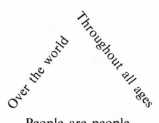

People are people

FIGURE 12: **Triangular Poem**

Poems may also be written in the shape of a circle, a parallelogram, or a spiral. They may also be made in the outlines of animals, trees, or people.

Noise Poems:

The themes for these poems are noises or the lack of noise. Pick a noise from inside, outside, or around the town.

Example:

I heard the birds flapping their wings.
They chirped their happiness.
America sings.

You may also play a record of various recorded sounds and have the students write a poem describing the noises or sounds.

Colorful Poems:

Poems may be written with a color in each line. A simple pattern is:

> Red is . . .
> Green is . . .
> When I think of blue, I see . . .

Relate the poems to expressions in the English language:

> green with envy
> wild blue yonder
> yellow rose of Texas
> yellow ribbon in the old oak tree

Haiku:

The haiku originated in Japan. It consists of a three-lined poem of 17 syllables. Line 1 contains five, Line 2 contains seven, Line 3 contains five syllables. The theme is usually nature.

Example:

> My rabbit Herbert—
> A friend in time of trouble—
> A pleasure for me.

Decorate the haiku with rice paper, which you can find in art stores.

Diamante:

The format for the diamante (diamond-shaped poem) is:

Line 1 — noun
Line 2 — two adjectives describing Line 1
Line 3 — three words ending in "-ing" (about Line 1)
Line 4 — four nouns about Line 1 or Line 7
Line 5 — three words ending in "-ing" (about Line 7)
Line 6 — two adjectives about Line 7
Line 7 — noun (can be opposite of Line 1)

Indians
brave, strong
working, hunting, fishing
food, clothing, shelter, life
starving, living, dying
ancient, proud
man

Colonists
strong, independent
fighting, starving, winning
tea, battles, freedom, life
ruling, leading, reigning
stately, proud
American

The poem may be written on a diamond-shaped piece of paper or on a kite.

Other Suggestions for Poetry:

1. Use words from songs to write poems. Write other words for the songs.
2. Take a famous poem and change the words.
3. Write poems with names of the students as the titles.
4. Make a list of the rhymes used in jumping rope.
5. Use nursery rhymes and have the students modernize the rhymes.
6. Set up a poetry center in the classroom.
7. Set up a bulletin board, "A POET — YOU KNOW IT."

POSTERS. Free and relatively inexpensive posters are available from a wide variety of sources. Some follow:

automobile dealers	barbershops	book stores
advertising agencies	beauty salons	bus companies
agricultural suppliers	beverage companies	camera shops
banks	boat dealers	clothing stores

colleges	gasoline stations	office equipment stores
drugstores	hardware companies	paint stores
employment agencies	health food stores	post office department
farms	insurance companies	restaurants
fishing dealers	labor unions	sporting goods stores
florists	lumber companies	supermarkets
furniture stores	newspapers	tire dealers

You may also find posters in magazines and in advertisements that come through the mail. Book clubs also have posters. Be on the alert for posters and charts for your classroom.

PRETENDING. The fun of pretending is sometimes lost by the time the students reach the school. They have "learned" to stifle part of their creativity and openness.

You can rekindle the pretending spirit in your students.

1. Put a movement record on the record player. Have the students move to the music. You should also move with them.

2. Have a student go before the class and portray a tree or another object. Have the other students guess the object.

3. Combine physical education and pretending. Have the students do exercises as if they were animals. Examples: walk like a duck, move like an elephant, crawl like a snake, hop like a kangaroo, charge like a bull.

4. Have the students pretend to be a famous person. Let the other students guess the identity of the mystery person.

5. Have the students write about the identity of an inanimate object. Tell the story from the object's point of view. Write a story about a pencil vs. the sharpener, shoes vs. feet, dirt vs. soap.

6. Have the students pretend that they're teacher for a day. You can also portray being a student. It will be very interesting to observe the students' reactions to the teacher.

7. Involve the students with career education and have them pretend to be people with different occupations. Have the other students guess the mystery occupations.

PROJECTIVE TECHNIQUES. Projective techniques are in-completed sentences used to determine feelings and attitudes of students. The students are presented with a variety of in-complete sentences and will complete them. The responses should be confidential.

You can determine many of the students' inner feelings. Do not try to psychoanalyze all the responses, but use them to help you to better understand the student.

1. Today I feel _____
2. When I have to read, I _____
3. I get angry when _____
4. School is _____
5. I wish my parents would _____
6. I can't understand why _____
7. Teachers are _____
8. I feel bad when _____
9. When I grow up, I _____
10. People think I _____
11. On weekends I _____
12. To me, homework is _____
13. I'm afraid of _____
14. When I take my report card home, I _____
15. When I do math, I _____
16. I would read more if _____
17. Comics _____
18. I wish I could _____
19. I wish someone would help me _____
20. I never would _____

Modify these or make up your own projective techniques.

PUZZLES. Puzzles have a learning function as well as an entertainment one. Puzzles can be used as an interest center and also as an art project.

1. Make a road map puzzle. Take a road map and mount it on a sheet of oak tag. Cut the map into pieces and put them in an envelope.

173

2. Wooden puzzles may be made with the help of the wood shop. You may also make puzzles from pressed wood. Cut the pieces with a jigsaw and put them in a frame.

3. To preserve a puzzle, put it together. Cover the back with white glue and mount it on a sheet of heavy cardboard.

4. Make a puzzle from the newspaper. Mount it on a sheet of oak tag. Leave several pieces of the puzzle in an envelope. Have the students guess what is written on the missing pieces.

5. Puzzles may be made of plexiglass and put in a frame.

6. Take a mathematics worksheet and cut it into the shape of a puzzle. Have the students solve the worksheet as they fix the puzzle.

7. Have the students make their own puzzles as part of a class art activity.

— stands for quadrilaterals, for historic quill pens, and for quizzes—sometimes too much a part of the learning process.

QUESTIONS. Questions. . .Questions. . .Questions! Good questioning techniques help to facilitate the teacher's role.

1. When asking a question, be ready to rephrase the question so that all the students comprehend it. Have the students respond to the question by changing the question into a statement.

2. When a child asks a question, present it to the entire class. Many of the students will have good answers. This is a possible lead-off to an effective discussion.

3. In order to introduce a unit of instruction, have the students write five or ten questions they would like to have answered. Use these as the basis for developing activities and experiences for the students.

4. Write WHO, WHAT, WHEN, WHERE, and WHY on a set of 3 x 5 cards. Write PEOPLE, ACTIONS, ADVERBS, PLACES, and REASONS on another set of cards. Have the students mix the two sets of cards and write a story about two cards.

5. Set up a "??????????? Center." Make up questions with a wide range of difficulty. The questions may vary from those with a *yes* or *no* answer to an in-depth question requiring research from several sources.

Example:

Does a cat breathe oxygen?
Which weighs more—a rhino or a hippo? (This may cause the students to ask other questions referring to the age or diet of the animals.)

6. Play the "Make a Match" game. Write clues to a question and have the students match the answers.

CLUE	WHO SAYS SO?
"May I help you?"	operator, salesperson
"Good morning, class."	teacher
"I like to eat my spinach."	Popeye
"Open your mouth wide!"	dentist
"Which record shall I play next?"	disc jockey
"Strike three! You're out!"	umpire

7. Play "The Answer Is." Write a series of possible answers to questions. Have the students make up the questions.

Answer list:

The White House	music
salad dressing	the Loch Ness Monster
cereal	snow
orange juice	tomorrow
I'm not afraid	sunshine
pink	Philadelphia
comic books	zebra

QUIET CENTER. A quiet center is a place where a child may sit and read or work quietly. The center is usually found in the corner of the classroom. A comfortable chair, mats, hassocks, or rugs help to make the center effective. It may be set apart from the classroom by a filing cabinet, room divider, or book shelf.

This area of the room provides the students with a great deal of freedom and also with the responsibility for behaving in a proper manner.

Reading materials that may be included in the center are comics, magazines, newspapers, paperback books, catalogs, and greeting cards. Writing materials should also be included. (See INTEREST CENTERS.)

— stands for rapport, for reinforcement of skills, and for readiness of the teacher and the student.

READING. The art of teaching students to read effectively is indeed a complex and difficult process. Some suggestions follow:

Consonants:

1. Set up a consonant table each week. Pick a letter and bring in objects and pictures beginning with the same consonant. Have the students write about the objects.

2. Have the students write words on cards. Organize them according to their initial consonants. Have the students classify the words into nouns, verbs, etc.

3. Make a category match game. Use various categories and have the students match the beginning consonants with the category.

Category	B	D	P
cars	Buick	Dodge	Plymouth
fruits	banana	date	peach
cities	Boston	Denver	Philadelphia

Consonant Blends:

1. Make a "blend tree." Find a tree branch and put it in a large can; fill the can with plaster of Paris. Have the students put words with consonant blends on the tree. Provide some samples of words with consonant blends.

2. Write a story about Sherman the Fresh Shrewd Shrimp. Make up similar sentences with consonant blends.

3. Make a list of names that contain blends. Find some famous people in American history with "blended" names.

4. Find ten cities or states with consonant blends—for example, Trenton, San Francisco, Florida.

5. Play "Consonant Continent." Make a map of the United States. Write the names of the states, omitting the consonants. Have the students complete the names.

Digraphs:

1. Make a digraph chart with examples and pictures:

"ch"—Cheerful Charlie   "gh"—Gerald Ghost
"ph"—Philadelphia Phil   "sh"—Shrewd Sharon
"th"—Thin Thelma   "wh"—Who the Whistler

2. Write sentences using digraph words:

The sharp whale whistled while the chicken threw the thin shell.

3. Write nonsense words phonetically. Have the students translate them.

ghly—fly   phlag—flag   whash—wash
whiphe—wife   ghit—fit   whith—with

4. Write a digraph paragraph. Have the students circle all the digraphs in the paragraph.

Vowels:

1. Play the "Vowel Towel" game. On a piece of unwoven cotton, print or embroider words with vowels of various pronunciations. Frame this and display it in the classroom.

2. Write the name of each student phonetically on a chart. Post the chart on the wall in a prominent spot.

3. Make a booklet to illustrate various phonetic rules and regulations. Include examples and sample sentences. Have the students decorate the booklets and keep them in their desks.

4. Make a vowel tree with ten branches—five for the long vowels and five for the short vowel sounds. Have the students write appropriate words to place on the tree.

5. Misspell some words on the blackboard or on a ditto. Have the students correct them.

prettee — pretty   heigh — hay   fewe — few

Prefixes:

The common prefixes and an example of each follow:

Prefix	Meaning	Example
ad-	to	adjoin
anti-	against	antislavery
bi-	two	bicycle
co-	together	cooperate
de-	remove	detach
in-	negative	inedible
inter-	between	international
intra-	within	intrastate
multi-	many	multisyllabic
non-	not	nonviolent
poly-	many	polysyllabic
pre-	before	prefix
quad-	four	quadruped
sub-	under	submarine
trans-	across	transportation

1. Select a prefix and develop a vocabulary lesson about it. Give the students the prefix of the word and the definition. Have them give you the word. This may be done orally or as part of a written assignment.

Prefix	Definition	Word
bi-	type of glasses	bifocals
bi-	with two motors	bimotored
de-	to reduce in grade	degrade
dis-	to uncover	disclose

ex-	to send to another country	export
fore-	to predict weather	forecast
in-	not considerate	inconsiderate
re-	to make known	reveal

2. Use these vocabulary words as the basis for the week's spelling list.

3. Use a basic root word and add as many prefixes as possible:

"port"—deport, export, import, report, support, transport.
"sent"—resent, dissent, absent, present, missent.
"mobile"—automobile, immobile.
"scribe"—describe, inscribe, prescribe, transcribe, proscribe, subscribe, circumscribe.

Suffixes:

Some common suffixes and examples follow:

Suffix	Meaning	Example
-able	able to	accountable
-age	general condition	tonnage
-dom	position	freedom
-en	made of	golden
-less	lacking	blameless
-ness	condition	kindness
-ship	office	leadership
-tion	result	generalization
-y	resembling	sunny

1. Have the students list as many words as they can with a given suffix:

"-less"—careless, needless, senseless, thoughtless, effortless.

2. Personalize some suffixes. Use them as topics for creative writing.

Larry Less	Abel Able	Izzie Ish
Sherman Ship	Loch Ness	Mo Tion

3. Make a puzzle that matches prefixes, root words, and suffixes. Put the puzzle pieces in manila envelopes.

(See CONTEXT, CRITICAL READING, and COMPREHENSION.)

RECORDS (PHONOGRAPH). Records provide many opportunities for creative learning and creative teaching.

1. Play a 45 rpm record at the proper speed and then at 78 or 33 ⅓. Have the students listen and discuss the differences.

2. Obtain an old 78 rpm record. Compare the type of music on the old record with today's music. Which record will last longer?

3. Teach a lesson to the class while a record is playing in the background. Have the students try to "tune out" the record player. Discuss the problems of doing homework with records playing. List the positive aspects of doing homework with records playing.

4. Discuss the process of record-making. Write a letter to a record company to find out the history of records.

5. Calculate the number of revolutions of a record in a given period of time.

33 ⅓ rpm	15 minutes	___revolutions
45 rpm	15 minutes	___revolutions
78 rpm	15 minutes	___revolutions

6. Play several new records and have the students rate them on the basis of 1 to 100. Average the scores to see which is the best. Keep track of the record on the radio stations.

7. Have the students bring in the "Top 10" list from the newspaper or record stores. Make a chart to keep track of the number of weeks a record remains in the "Top 10."

8. Copy the lyrics to a song and analyze them. Have the students write new lyrics for the song.

9. Allow the students to bring in records as a part of your music instruction. Bring in some of your favorite records and play them for the class.

RECORDS (SCHOOL AND CLASSROOM). The task of record-keeping frequently presents problems. These problems may be solved by:

1. Using a file box as an anecdotal record. Write comments and suggestions for further reference.

2. Ditto a class list and refer to this for keeping track of the students' work.

3. Make a loose-leaf notebook with a page for each child. Use this to record levels of progress. This format allows a great amount of flexibility. Keep samples of students' work in the notebook.

REWARDS. Rewards provide a needed incentive and motivation in order to stimulate learning.

A project that works well in this area is a series of coupon rewards. See Figure 13. (The name "Cotlersville Coupons" was selected by the students.) The coupons shown here were printed at a professional print shop, but they may be duplicated on a ditto master.

As the students complete specific assignments, they are given a coupon. Coupons may be used to motivate assignments in mathematics, to improve student behavior, or in any other subject matter area.

Cotlersville Coupons may be redeemed for increased physical education time, puzzles, paperback books, "gum day" (in which the students may chew gum in school), free time, or other rewards.

The students participate in establishing the rules and regulations regarding the use of the coupons.

ROLE PLAYING. Role playing may become an integral part of the language arts, social studies, or affective education program. The teacher literally establishes the key role in this area. The attitude of the teacher toward creative role playing will have a definite effect upon the students.

FIGURE 13: Cotlersville Coupons

1. Switch the roles of teacher and student for a lesson. Have a student teach the class. You act like a student. Discuss the changes in the roles.

2. Make a list of roles to play. Some could be George Washington, the Statue of Liberty, doctor, lawyer, Indian chief, singer, and author. Have a student go in front of the class and portray a role. Let the rest of the class guess what role he is playing.

3. Hold a round-table discussion to discuss the changing roles of men and women in society. Make a list of the areas that

have changed over the years. Create a "Changing Role Bulletin Board."

4. Make a collage of various occupations throughout history. Make it into a "Before and Now" display.

— stands for satisfactory; for the seashore—a nice place to visit; and for school—one place where education and fun *can* happen.

SCIENCE. Individual topics under the general category of science are discussed throughout the book. (See ANIMALS, BULLETIN BOARDS, CAMERA, ECOLOGY, ENRICH-MENT, FUTURE, HOROSCOPE, INQUIRY, INTEREST CENTERS, MACHINES, NEWSPAPERS, PLANTS, SEASONS, SPACE, VOLCANOES, and WEATHER.)

SEASONS. The four seasons provide the elementary educator with innumerable possibilities.

1. Make a word play game using the four seasons. How many words can your students make from "winter, spring, summer, fall"?

2. Take a picture of a scene during each of the four seasons. Have the students identify the correct season and give reasons for their selections.

3. Have the students experience the arrival of the various seasons. On the first day of winter, have them go outside and use their senses to detect the signs of winter. Do this for the other times of the year.

4. Make a list of sports played during the various seasons. Which ones are only played during one season of the year? Which ones continue through the seasons? Make a chart to describe this.

5. Have a contest to guess the day that will have the first snowfall, first shower in April, first day of 32° weather, etc. This will be adapted to your part of the country.

6. Make a calendar based on *The Farmer's Almanac.* Indicate the time to plant vegetables and fruit in your specific geographical area.

7. Have the students find different meanings for the words *winter, spring, summer,* and *fall.*

Example:

> spring—part of an automobile.
> fall—part of a wrestling match.

8. Use a foreign language to provide an equivalent for our words:

> winter—invierno
> spring—primavera
> summer—verano
> fall—otoño

9. Compare seasons in North American to seasons in South America.

10. Make a list of all the *season*-ings used in cooking. Find out which are roots, seeds, bark, and leaves.

11. Locate several songs by The Four Seasons. Play them in a listening center activity.

The following activities will vary depending upon your grade level and geographical location. They will also change with the weather.

Winter:

1. If a snow falls, have the students study the flakes. Take black construction paper outside and allow it to cool, then collect some snowflakes on it and observe them outside. Draw them when you return to the classroom.

2. Keep track of the temperature each day for the months of January, February, and March. Compare this to November

and December temperatures. Calculate the average for the months. Make a chart to compare results.

3. Set up a display of winter clothing. Make a psychedelic snowman and dress him in the clothing. Use for creative writing activities.

Spring:

1. During an early spring shower, take the students outside. Let them feel the rain. Discuss their feelings after the experience.

2. Write a poem based on "Spring is..." Illustrate it.

3. Select a mountain in the United States or in another country. Write a story about "Springtime in the————"

4. Begin your plant unit. Have the students plant a garden near the school.

Summer:

1. Have the students plan some worthwhile learning activities during the summer.

2. Plan an imaginary vacation to a famous resort during the summer. Let the students develop an itinerary. Write for brochures to the resort area.

3. Compare the various types of recreation throughout the world. What areas have summer weather throughout the year?

4. Make up a crossword puzzle with summer terms. Some are:

seashore	fun	boating	vacation	scuba
fishing	baseball	play	swimming	visit

Fall:

1. Make a football bulletin board. Have the students add pictures and articles to the display.

2. Make a list of words from "Autumn time = fun time."

3. Write a story that compares fall in Hawaii to fall in Alaska.

4. Make projects with leaves. Observe them, trace them, write poems about them, make leaf fossils with plaster of Paris.

SELF-CONCEPT. A child's self-concept or self-image is a result of the child's heredity and environment.

Here are several ways to help improve students' self-concepts. You can also use this list for your own self-evaluation.

1. Never embarrass a child in front of the class.
2. Make special efforts to accept the child's individuality and special modes of learning.
3. Praise the child when needed. Do not be false in praise.
4. Make a list of positive comments about each child. Keep the list for conferences and record cards.
5. Never talk about a child in front of other teachers. Keep the child's behavior a confidential matter between appropriate individuals.
6. Show the students respect at all times. A mutual respect between teacher and student will result.
7. Make special efforts to remember birthdays or special achievements of the students. Send birthday cards and little notes to reward outstanding achievement.
8. Hold rap sessions to improve situations in the classroom.
9. Try to recall being a student. It will help you realize some of your students' problems.

SLIDES. Slides may be used to instruct and also to recall special events or programs. They are relatively inexpensive as compared to photographs.

1. Make a slide show combined with the presentation of oral reports. Using slide film, take a picture of each child. Tape record the students' oral reports. As the tape of a child is being played, project his picture onto a screen.

2. Write-on slides are available from audio-visual dealers or camera stores. These slides contain a film that can be used to

create your own slides. Use a pen, pencil overhead marker, or permanent marker to create a slide.

These slides may be used for vocabulary development, mathematical facts, creating pictures and special effects, teaching map skills, and for following directions.

3. Use a combination of photographic slides and write-on slides to make a slide presentation. In one of my classes the students illustrated several slides to go with the song "Big Yellow Taxi." Other photographic slides were mixed with the write-on ones. They were placed in a sequential order and shown while the record was playing.

4. Another way to make slides is with a special commercially prepared slide maker. It consists of a camera with a special lens, a stand to support the camera, and a frame for students' work. This slide maker is effective for creating original slides. Check with your camera store for more specific information.

5. People who have traveled to a foreign country or to various places in America may be willing to share their slides and experiences with your class.

6. Prepared slides and/or tape programs are frequently available from museums, local libraries, governmental agencies, manufacturing companies, and historical societies. These may be obtained either free or at a nominal cost, which may include return postage.

7. Commercially prepared slides on a wide variety of topics are available, either individually or in sets, from the major audio-visual companies. Write for free catalogs.

SLOW LEARNER. The slow learner is found in all learning situations. The basic definition of the slow learner with specific learning problems will vary within school systems or states. However, they may be grouped into several categories. They are: Gross Motor, Sensory-Motor, Perceptual Motor, Language, Conceptual, and Social.

Each category will be briefly discussed. Several suggestions will be given for each category.

Gross Motor: This area involves the development of large muscle activity.

1. Exercises including rolling, balancing, walking, running, skipping, jumping, dancing, and movement in different ways are recommended.
2. An obstacle course may be established to improve skills.
3. The child should be talked to in order to relieve some anxiety.

Sensory-Motor: This area involves the psycho-physical blending of fine and gross motor activities.

1. Some exercises for this area include balancing, bouncing, throwing a ball, following directions, and coordination skills.
2. The child is given practice in copying the assignments from the blackboard.
3. Directions must be specific and completely understood by the students.

Perceptual Motor: This area involves the auditory, visual, and visual-motor skills.

1. The child should be given problems dealing with association of words, auditory memory, and auditory discrimination.
2. The child should also be helped with his visual acuity and visual memory.
3. Direction-following activities are needed.
4. Move the child to a seat near you. Give individual and specific directions to him.
5. If the child has a hearing problem, practice dictation, use the tape recorder, and exaggerate your speech pattern.

6. Use magazine pictures to make a puzzle. Have the child complete the puzzle.
7. If possible, work on a one-to-one level.

Language: This area includes the child's psycho-linguistic development.

1. Accept the child's best language only.
2. Use the tape recorder to improve instruction.
3. Make the child aware of the listening audience.
4. Important areas include vocabulary development, sentence sense, word attack skills, reading comprehension, and articulation.
5. Writing, spelling, and handwriting development are also important here. Point out errors and make suggestions for improvement.

Conceptual Skills: This area involves the general reasoning ability and the attainment of concepts.

1. Be concrete in dealing with mathematical concepts. The child is not at the abstract level of instruction.
2. Set small, achievable tasks for the child.
3. Use money to teach addition, subtraction, and figuring change.
4. Make several classifying tasks for the child to achieve.
5. Check the child's comprehension of the given skills.
6. Review previous skills and provide reinforcement activities.

Social Acceptance: This area involves problem-solving and social relationships.

1. Have the child make an "All About Me" poster.
2. Help the child to keep a diary.
3. Praise the child frequently for his positive behavior.
4. Use a story approach to develop values. Give the child a situation and discuss the values inherent in the story.

To be successful with an exceptional child, work closely with the child study team, the parents, and the child himself.

Find out all you can about him. Encourage success and he will succeed.

The instruction of slow learners must be individualized. Above all, *teach* the slow learner. He will not learn merely by being in the classroom. He needs to be effectively taught.

SPACE. The planets and the solar system are topics that students enjoy. This may be taught at all grade levels.

1. Make a chart of the planets. Have the students fill in the various information including the name of the planet, its satellites, distance from the sun, length of the year, and other pertinent information.

2. Make up a sentence beginning with the first letter of each planet. The order is from the sun to the outer planets.

My very elderly moose just sat upon nine pineapples.

3. Make papier mache models of the planets. Suspend them as mobiles in the classroom.

4. Plan an imaginary trip to one of the planets. Have the students make a list of all the items they would like to take along with them. Plan the trip for a year.

5. Have the students watch a space show or cartoon on television. Analyze the show to determine what aspects may become realities.

6. Make a representation of the distance between the planets. Do this on the playground with a scale of 1 ft. = 1 million miles. Have the students portray the planets and the sun.

7. Write letters to the Federal Government to find out more information about space programs.

8. Organize a rocket club in your classroom. Information is available from hobby shops.

9. Hold a round-table discussion to determine if there is life on other planets.

10. Keep track of UFO's (Unidentified Flying Objects) in the newspaper and other media.

11. Make a list of space vocabulary for the students to define: asteroid, shooting stars, meteors, meteroids, and comets.

12. Have the students demonstrate a lunar and a solar eclipse.

13. Look up the origin of the planets. Find the names in Roman and Greek mythology.

14. Look up the history of telescopes and the early astronomers.

15. Make models of satellites with aluminum foil. Display throughout the classroom.

16. Look up the history of rockets—from the early Chinese to modern times.

17. Make a list of dangerous situations that could occur on a space flight to a mystery planet.

18. Design a space ship for the future.

19. Write reports about famous astronauts.

20. Make up a name for a new planet. Hold a contest for the suggestion of the best one.

SPELLING.   The basic spelling program consists of a basal text and routine procedures. The words are introduced, written several times, used in sentences or definitions, and tested on Friday.

These suggestions will put more life into your spelling program:

1. Select spelling words from the reading books, social studies text, science book, and special events.

2. Play "Spelling Baseball." The rules of baseball apply, and the difficulty of the words determines singles, doubles, etc.

3. Have the students select their own words from various sources. They will frequently choose words which are more difficult than those presented in the text.

4. Set up a "buddy system" for finding errors in assignments.

5. Keep a list of misspelled words that you find in the newspaper.

6. Hold an old-fashioned spelling bee.

7. Have a "Mis-spelling Day." On any one day of the week, make several spelling mistakes. Observe whether the students will correct the mistakes.

8. Make up a worksheet with every word misspelled. Spell the words phonetically correct. As a follow-up activity, have the students also make up a misspelled worksheet. They must provide the correct answers.

9. Make spelling cards with glitter or colored sand. Display them throughout the room.

SPORTS. The sports scene allows individual needs to be effectively met. It also provides an alternative to learning.

Social Studies:

1. Research the history of various sports. Trace the changes that have taken place over the years.

2. Do an in-depth study of the Olympic Games. Divide the topic to cover specific periods of time or specific countries.

3. Compare the national sports of Europe and Latin America to those of our country. Why are they different?

4. Make a list of participation sports and observation sports. What are the reasons for the differences?

Language Arts:

1. Have the students write a letter to a local baseball, basketball, or football team, asking for information. Letters may be sent to teams at the high school, college, or professional level.

2. Write a news article about the events on your school playground. Incorporate this as part of a classroom or school newspaper.

3. Write the directions for playing a game. Follow the directions exactly and determine if the game can be played from the students' directions.

4. Make up your own game. Design a place for the game, list the directions, and list the equipment needed to play it.

5. Make a list of specialized vocabulary words used in sports. Have the students define the words according to the dictionary. They can then define the words according to the specifics of the game. Make a matching game with the words:

Word		Sport
"icing"	—	ice hockey
"bucket"	—	basketball
"red dog"	—	football
"butterfly"	—	swimming
"birdie"	—	golf
"frame"	—	bowling
"scratch"	—	horse racing

6. Observe a sports event on television. Listen carefully to the words of the commentators. Compare your reactions to theirs.

Mathematics:

1. Have the students write mathematical problems dealing with various sports. Put them on cards and have the students make up an answer key. Set these up in a mathematics center.

2. Relate the shapes of fields and playing surfaces to geometry: football field — rectangle; baseball — diamond; etc.

3. To illustrate graphs, have the students keep track of a team's win/loss record.

4. Establish a "Guess Who Sunday's Winners Will Be" contest. Put the names of the football teams on a bulletin board. Have the students select the winners. Keep track of the percentages right and wrong.

5. Have the students bring in the sports section of the newspaper. Figure averages of various sports as a math assignment.

Science:

1. Perform experiments with various pieces of equipment to determine if the weights and dimensions are exactly what they are supposed to be.

2. Perform a scientific test to see which ball bounces the highest—baseball, basketball, tennis ball, volley ball, etc.

3. Discuss the use of friction in sports—ice skating, automobile racing, and skiing.

4. Discuss the effects of rain and snow on various events.

Physical Education:

Perhaps the most important area of sports involvement is the gymnasium and the playground.

1. Have each child who is physically able, participate in all activities.

2. Have the students who are less capable in athletics work with more capable students. This will help to develop a cooperative feeling among the students.

3. Have each student in the class become captain of a team. Set up a rotating schedule so that each child can serve in the leadership role.

4. In a game of kickball, have the boys play the girls. In the next game, mix the teams. Compare the differences between the games.

5. Participate in the activities with the students.

SPRING FEVER. Spring Fever can occur—

> on a warm January day...
> before, during, and after spring vacation...
> in September...

How to fight (or live with) Spring Fever:

1. When the weather becomes unseasonably warm, take the class outside and hold a lesson. A shady tree or a shaded side of the building will help.

2. Change the schedule during the day. The alternating of various subjects may help to maintain student interest.

3. Extend the physical education period for a few minutes.

4. Increase the number of art projects.

5. Take a walking field trip around the school. Have the students become aware of new or different sights around the school's environment.

6. Use math and language games to motivate the students.

7. Have the students make projects and present oral reports. The topics for the projects and reports can be of the students' choosing.

8. Devote a part of each day to reading a book to the class. Suggested good times for this are before lunch and after physical education period. It will give the students several minutes to sit quietly and listen.

STAMPS (POSTAGE). Postage stamps may be used:

1. To teach the history of the country by collecting various historical stamps. Kits are available at the post office.

2. On an inquiry basis. Give the students stamps from a foreign country. Have them analyze the stamps to determine clues about the foreign countries.

3. To teach about famous people. Many stamps commemorate famous people and their accomplishments. Locate the biographies of these individuals and make a project.

4. To develop an interest in philately.

5. To learn about the "Stamp Acts."

6. To teach mathematics. Have the students research the costs of various types of postage and the costs of the stamps throughout the years.

7. To motivate art projects. Have the students design original stamps.

SUBSTITUTES. Substitutes provide a needed service for the teacher and the school system. To insure the maximum use of substitutes, the teacher must provide a basic guide for the substitute.

The guide may include:

1. Seating chart that is current.
2. Lists of rules and regulations for the class.
3. Special procedures for your students.
4. Schedules of special teachers and the schedule of the subjects.
5. List of all the students in the class.
6. Location of attendance cards, lunch count forms, etc.
7. List of specific texts and pages in books and workbooks.
8. A set of general activities to be done in case the substitute completes all the assignments early.
9. An evaluation sheet for the substitute to complete. This should include:

   > Name of substitute
   > lessons completed (for each subject)
   > comments
   > special problems

In order to insure effective substitutes, relate any problems to the principal so that he is aware of them. In this way, both the substitute and the school will benefit.

SYNONYMS.   Synonyms are words with the same or similar meanings.

1. Make a Synonym City. Have the students put in streets and their synonyms. Every person's occupation has a synonym. Everything within the city has a synonym. Make a poster or diagram of your city.

2. Have the students select a word such as "walk." Have the students list as many as possible synonyms for the word. Use the word as both a noun and a verb. This will encourage the students to use both the dictionary and the thesaurus.

3. As new vocabulary words are developed, keep a synonym list on a sheet of paper. Use the list to reinforce the words.

4. Set up a synonym center. Attach a series of words and have the students find their synonyms. Change the words each week. (See Figure 14.)

FIGURE 14: Synonym Sue

— stands for toil and trouble, which are sometimes a part of the learning process; for time (a lack of which is always present); and for teachers, of course.

TAPE RECORDER.   The tape recorder can become your friend and helping hand if you use it properly.

1. Record a lesson and analyze it. Listen for pronunciation, for variance in pitch, for enthusiasm, and for expression. It is a good self-teaching experience for the teacher.

2. Develop listening activities. Record a set of directions with some background noise. Have the students listen carefully and follow the appropriate directions.

3. Record stories from the reading book or other books. Categorize the tapes and store them in a special area. You may want to cooperate with another teacher on this project.

4. Record sounds around the home and the school. Have the students identify them. *Examples:*

car engine	leaves rustling
doorbell	motorcycle
farm sounds	pinball machine
hammer/anvil	running water

5. Have the students record sounds around the school.

6. Record a baseball game. Ask the students questions about the game. Set this up as a listening center.

7. Have the students tape record a story or poems for another class.

8. Record lessons for students who are having difficulty reading the textbook.

TASK CARDS. Task cards are also known as job cards, interest center activities, activity cards, or assignments.

They may be made on index cards, on sheets of tag board, or on pieces of paper. Laminating helps to preserve the cards.

Here is a sample activity card:

A Purple Cow in Your Garden   Creative Writing/Art

You have just planted a garden near your house. A purple cow has entered your garden.

1. Tell what you would do to remove the cow from the garden.

2. Draw a purple cow.

Guidelines for Task Cards:
1. The title should attract the attention of the student.
2. The specific subjects for the card should be listed on it.
3. The directions should be clear and specific. The students should know exactly what is expected of them.
4. The cards may include art work or pictures of various objects.
5. Task cards may be used with all grade levels.
6. They may be used in all subject matter areas.
7. Students may assist in making task cards for other students.

TELEVISION. Television is one of today's most influential media. Some students watch television for as much as five hours a day.

1. Find other words beginning with "tele-." *Examples:* telephone, telegraph, teleprompter. Have the students define them.

2. Write a letter to a major television broadcast station for information about specific programs.

3. Make a list of the students' favorite television shows. Chart the results.

4. Use the program listing to develop activities for the class.

- What appears on Channel 99 at 7:30 AM?
- How many hours of news are on a certain channel each day?
- How many commercials do the stations average an hour?
- Calculate the number of cartoons that appear on Saturday morning.

5. Compare the public broadcasting system to one of the national networks.

6. Adapt some of the television games for classroom use.

7. Make a list of the types of programs that appear in the morning and in the afternoon. Compare.

8. Make a television guessing game. Write questions that may be answered by the names of television shows or characters.

Who is a Pink Feline?   ("Pink Panther)
Who is on a very expensive show? ("The Six Million Dollar Man")

9. Watch the cartoons on Saturday or Sunday morning. Develop creative writing activities based on them.

10. Obtain an old TV cabinet and make it into a puppet theater.

11. Make models of television sets from cardboard.

12. Find out the cost of an advertisement on a television station.

TEXTBOOKS. Textbooks are a basis for public school teaching. They can be used or abused by the teacher.

1. Have the students read a selection. Select one student to answer questions posed by other students. Have him go to the front of the class. The other students will ask him questions based on the selection. As long as the student answers correctly, he remains before the class. If he makes a mistake, the questioner gives an answer and the two change places.

2. Use the textbook as a resource, not as an ultimate answer. Find several texts dealing with the same topic. Have the students compare the material and its presentation.

3. Have the students re-write a portion of a text. Emphasize preciseness of thought, accuracy, and readability.

4. Use old and discarded textbooks as supplemental materials. Cut them up for interest centers and worksheets for the students. Foreign language students provide novel approaches in this area.

TRANSPARENCIES. In addition to acetate sheets, transparencies may be made with clear Con-Tact paper.

1. Place a piece of clear Con-Tact paper on a picture from a magazine. Clay based pictures work the best. To determine if the picture is clay based, wet and rub the picture. If the paper rubs off easily, it is probably clay based. Use a small portion of the picture.

2. Rub the Con-Tact paper and picture with a scissors handle or paper clip. This will make the Con-Tact paper stick well.

3. Soak the covered picture in warm, soapy water until the paper is thoroughly soaked.

4. Peel the paper, dry, and use on an overhead projector.

5. Experiment with various pictures for best results.

TRANSPORTATION. Transportation is a unit that may be developed at both primary and elementary levels.

1. Define *transportation*. Find other words which use the prefix "trans-" and the root word "port."

2. Construct a chart tracing the history of transportation from the caveman era to modern times.

3. Compare animals' means of transportation to man's. How many animals have inspired man's inventions?

> birds — flying
> armadillo — armored tanks
> ducks — swimming fins

4. Find out the speeds of various animals in the encyclopedia. Make a chart comparing them.

5. Find special means of transportation throughout the world. Have the students construct models of these modes of travel.

> dog sled   ox cart   rickshaw   kayak   outrigger

6. Have the students design a new means of travel. It should be capable of air, land, and sea travel.

7. Write letters to major automobile, airline, and steamship companies for pictures and information about their companies.

8. Which animals today are still beasts of burden? In which countries are these animals found?

> elephant   ox   water buffalo   camels

9. Obtain pictures of new cars from automobile dealers. Use these to make a collage. Compare the prices and the equipment on various new cars.

10. Design a transportation system for congested cities. Include new buses and transportation (rapid) systems. Write letters to the public transportation system to find out their ideas for the future.

TYPEWRITER. A typewriter in the classroom can be used in all areas of the curriculum.

1. Obtain an old typewriter from a repair shop. The repair shops may have several that cannot be repaired. Allow the students to take the typewriter apart. Be sure to supervise the project.

2. Set up a portable typewriter in a corner of the room. Include various types of paper, pens, pencils, and erasers. Allow the students to type reports, projects, and poetry, or to work on newspapers.

3. Set up a schedule of perhaps one-half hour so that each student will have a chance to use the typewriter.

— stands for the mythical creature, the Unicorn; for urgent—which many problems appear to be; and for understanding.

UNITS OF STUDY.   Units of study may last from one week to as many as eight weeks, depending upon the topic and the grade level.

They help the teacher to organize a given part of the curriculum. They also may be revised or changed over a period of time.

The basic parts of a unit of study include:
1. A specific topic.
2. The time needed to complete the unit.
3. Grade level of the unit.
4. Behavioral objectives—general and specific.
5. Basic content or subject matter to be covered.
6. Activities—introductory, developmental, and culminating.
7. Resources for the unit—films, filmstrips, charts, maps, posters, multimedia kits, records, tapes, etc.
8. Bibliography—for teachers and for students.
9. Evaluation devices.

Units of study may be commercially prepared or teacher made. They are also available from several encyclopedia companies.

— stands for versatile (which teachers must be); for vim and vigor (needed to maintain the teaching schedule); and for violence, which has no place in schools.

VALUES. Teachers teach values by their examples as well as by planned teaching experiences.

The values you hold as a teacher are frequently transferred to the students.

1. *The value of honesty.* You may tell students that they should be honest, but telling is not sufficient.

Place a box with $2.00 or $3.00 in change in a special part of the room. Allow the students to borrow and repay as needed.

Use the money as the basis for an honor system. Observe the results of the experiment. Hold a discussion to evaluate the success of the project.

2. *The value of personal property.* Stage an incident in the classroom in which several students argue over who owns an object. Have the class decide who should have the object. Allow the class to offer several alternatives to solve the problem.

3. Make up a series of situation cards with an unfinished story as the format. Have the students discuss the problems and offer solutions.

A child forgets his report card and is caught by the teacher.
A child observes another stealing something from the teacher.
Someone finds $10.00 in the classroom.

A judge is accused of taking a bribe.
A child lies to the principal and is suspended.

VOCABULARY. Vocabulary development is an integral part of the reading program and also an important component in a child's success in school.

1. Put a new word on the board each day. Use it in a sentence; use it at least three times that day; put it on a chart. Review the words each day. Have the students do the same. This will insure the exposing of several hundred new words to the students.

2. Pick a page of the dictionary. Read the words to the students. Have them select one and include it as a part of the spelling program.

3. Make new words by adding prefixes and suffixes. Vary the tenses of verbs and the forms of nouns. Build on words that the students already know.

4. Develop worksheets using context clues to develop vocabulary.

5. Take a specific occupation and make a list of its jargon. Have the students define the words and use them in sentences. Do this on a weekly basis.

6. Find foreign words that have become a part of our language.

7. Use the newspaper and other printed material as a basis for increasing vocabulary.

8. Find words that have slang origins—AWOL, boloney, snafu.

9. Make a list of new words that have appeared in the last few years. How many of these words are a part of the students' vocabulary?

VOLCANO. Volcanoes may be made during a study of many countries throughout the world. They are also appropriate during a study of the earth and geography.

Take a can and build a plaster of Paris volcano around it. After the plaster has dried, paint with tempera or spray paint.

Use a baking soda and vinegar mixture to explode the volcano.

Ammonium dichromate may also be used. However, the ashes from burning ammonium dichromate may irritate the skin.

A volcano-making contest may be held in your class. (See HAWAII.)

— is for wampum; for wheels (large and small); and for wishes, which may come true.

WEATHER. The daily changes in the weather are a good way to involve the students in a scientific study.

1. Obtain a weather map or computer read-out from a local weather service. Post this in the room and place the various symbols on the map.

2. Compare the weather forecasts on television with the actual weather outside. Calculate the percentage of correct predictions.

3. Make up figures of people for various types of weather or weather terms:

Anna Mometer   Hy Grometer   Fogg E. Day
Hy Lowe   Wind E. Front   Typhoon O. Tornado

4. Set up a weather vane outside your classroom. Observe the wind directions. If possible, locate an antique weather vane. Bring it in and have the students illustrate it.

5. Do an in-depth study of the causes of weather.

6. Observe and illustrate various types of clouds. Make a chart comparing the clouds and the type of weather that accompanies each.

7. Find expressions that go with the weather:

Cats and dogs
Fair weather friends

— stands for xylophone; for *X* as in *X* marks the spot; and for *X* as the unknown part of life.

 — stands for youth (which never ends while going though it and which is remembered affectionately by those who have gone through it); for Yankee Doodle; and for yellow, a lovely color.

 — is for zeal; for the zenith of the educational process; and for zero—a circle with no beginning or no end. The education of children begins with *YOU* and has no end.

ZIP CODE, U.S.A. Each state of the United States has a two-letter abbreviation for Zip Code purposes. The activity described here will make the students aware of the abbreviations in a "fun" way.

Place the Zip Code abbreviations on the board or duplicate them for the students. Then ask the students to answer the questions. The answer to each of the questions is the abbreviation for one of the states. (After the students have answered these questions they may make up their own.)

The abbreviations and questions follow:

ZIP CODE ABBREVIATIONS

ALABAMA	AL	MONTANA	MT
ALASKA	AK	NEBRASKA	NB
ARIZONA	AZ	NEVADA	NV
ARKANSAS	AR	NEW HAMPSHIRE	NH
CALIFORNIA	CA	NEW JERSEY	NJ
COLORADO	CO	NEW MEXICO	NM
CONNECTICUT	CT	NEW YORK	NY
DELAWARE	DE	NORTH CAROLINA	NC
DISTRICT OF		NORTH DAKOTA	ND
COLUMBIA	DC	OHIO	OH
FLORIDA	FL	OKLAHOMA	OK
GEORGIA	GA	OREGON	OR
HAWAII	HI	PENNSYLVANIA	PA
IDAHO	ID	PUERTO RICO	PR
ILLINOIS	IL	RHODE ISLAND	RI
INDIANA	IN	SOUTH CAROLINA	SC
IOWA	IA	SOUTH DAKOTA	SD
KANSAS	KS	TENNESSEE	TN
KENTUCKY	KY	TEXAS	TX
LOUISIANA	LA	UTAH	UT
MAINE	ME	VERMONT	VT
MARYLAND	MD	VIRGINIA	VA
MASSACHUSETTS	MA	VIRGIN ISLANDS	VI
MICHIGAN	MI	WASHINGTON	WA
MINNESOTA	MN	WEST VIRGINIA	WV
MISSISSIPPI	MS	WISCONSIN	WI
MISSOURI	MO	WYOMING	WY

ENCYCLOPEDIC DESKBOOK OF TEACHING IDEAS AND CLASSROOM ACTIVITIES

by HAROLD I. COTLER

Here's a complete A-to-Z listing of projects, bulletin boards, lesson plans and field trips that can help you effectively plan and organize methods of instruction that suit your needs. Through these hundreds of practical, useful and tested techniques, your class will become highly motivated and eager for learning—meaning less discipline problems and less class preparation time for you!

PARTIAL OUTLINE OF ENTRIES

Achievement
Action Words
Activity Day
Advertisements
Animals
Art Projects
Awards
Behavior
Book Fair
Brainstorming
Bulletin Boards
Calendar Activities
Camera
Career Education
Community Resources
Conferences
Creative Writing
Decision-Making
Dictionary Games
Discipline
Diversity
Drug Education
Ecology
Economics
Emotions

Ethnic Studies
Exercises
Field Trips
Flashcards
Folklore
Geography
Grammar
Guidance
Holidays
Homework
Indians
Interest Centers
Junk
Kits
Lesson Plans
Library
Limericks
Machines
Magazines
Maps
Mathematics
Metrics
Mobiles
Motivation
Music

Newspapers
Open House
Organization
Photography
Physical Education
Plants
Poetry
Posters
Puzzles
Questions
Reading
Rewards
Role Playing
Seasons
Self-Concept
Slides
Slow Learner
Spelling
Sports
Spring Fever
Tape Recorder
Television
Values
Weather
Zip Code

ABOUT THE AUTHOR

HAROLD I. COTLER is currently an elementary teacher at the Winslow School in Vineland, New Jersey. In addition, he is an Adjunct Professor of Elementary Education at Glassboro State College, Glassboro, New Jersey. In 1973 he was awarded a Mini Grant from the New Jersey Department of Education for "SPARK '73,"—School Program for an Alternative Road to Knowledge. Mr. Cotler is the author of two specialized activity packages for New Jersey and Pennsylvania schools, and has conducted several teacher workshops. He is enrolled in a Doctoral Program in Curriculum and Instruction at Temple University.

Answer the following questions with a Zip Code abbreviation:

1. Which state is a boy's name — AL
2. Which two states spell a Bible name?   CA+IN=CAIN
3. What did Morse develop? (2 states)   CO+DE = CODE
4. Which two states did come?   CA+ME = CAME
5. What is the past tense of make? (2 states)

    MA+DE = MADE

6. If it's not AC it's ...   DC
7. Antonym of out is..   IN
8. What is a hot drink? (2 times)   CO+CO = COCO
9. What is the sixth note of the scale?   LA
10. Which state is a doctor?   MD
11. My mother is called...   MA
12. Which state is not well?   IL
13. Which state is a girl?   VI, or PA+ME+LA=PAMELA
14, Who likes women's lib?   MS
15. Which state is an exclamation?   OH
16. Which state is a conjunction?   OR
17. Do, Re, ...   MI
18. Ma likes ...   PA or ME
19. Which state asks a question?   WI or WY
20. Which state is all right?   OK
21. Which state says hello?   HI
22. What is the abbreviation for month?   MO
23. What is the number 6 in Roman numerals?   VI
24. Show me your identification...   ID
25. Which state is a kind of bread?   RI

Index

A

Abbreviations, 53
Achievement, 15
Achievement motivation, 16
Achievement tests, 16-17
Action words, 17-18
Activities:
    do it yourself, 55-56
    enrichment, 66-67
Activity day, 18
Adjectives, 88
Adverbs, 89
Advertisements, 19
Affective education, 19-20
Aides (instructional), 20
Aids, audio-visual, 20-21
Air pollution, 61
Aloha Game, 83
Animals, 21-22
Antonyms, 22-23
Art projects, 23-24, 56
Audio-visual aids, 20-21
Awards, 24-25

B

Behavior, 26-27
Book fair, 27
Book reports, 27-28
Books, 28-29
Brainstorming, 29
Bulletin boards, 29-32

C

Calendar activities, 33-34
Camera, 34
Card catalog system, 55
Card file, 56
Career education, 35-36
Centers:
    interest, 110-114
    listening, 123
    quiet, 176-177
Change of hearts, 57
Charts, 36
Cities, 85
Civil War, 97
Climate, 84
Cognitive education, 19
Colonial history, 95-96
Columbus, 94-95
Community resources, 36-37
Competition, 37
Comprehension, 37-38
Concepts, 38-39
Conceptual skills, slow learner, 192
Conferences (parent-teacher):
    conference itself, 40-41
    follow-up, 41
    pre-planning, 39-40
Conjunctions, 89
Consonant blends, 178-179
Consonants, 178
Context, 41-42
Contracts (learning), 42, 43

Conversation, 42-44
Creative writing, 44-45
Creativity:
    students, 46-47
    teacher, 46
Critical reading, 47
Curiosity, 47-48
Curriculum, 48

D

Decision-making process, 49
Democracy, 49-50
Developmental tasks, 50-51
Diagnosis, 51
DICTIONARY, 53
Dictionary games, 51-53
Dictionary Race, 52
Digraphs, 179
Dioramas, 53-54
Directions, geography, 85
Discipline, 54
Ditto masters, 56
Diversity, 55
Dollar bill inquiry, 56
Dramatics, 56-57
Dropouts, 57-58
Drug education, 58-59

E

Earth's surface, 82, 84
Earth-sun relationships, 85
Ecology:
    air pollution, 61
    concepts, 60
    inside classroom, 63-64
    land, 61-62
    nature, 60-61
    sound, 63
    water, 62-63
Economic education, 64-65
Education:
    affective, 19-20
    economics, 64-65
    environmental, 60-64 (*see also*
        Ecology)
    physical, 165-166

Emotion, 65-66
Emotional development, 51
Enrichment activities, 66-67
Environmental education, 60-64 (*see also*
        Ecology)
Ethnic studies, 67-69
Etymology, 69-70
Evaluation, 70-71
Exercises, 71
Experiments, 71-72

F

Fall, 188-189
Feelings, 73
Field trips, 74
Films, 74-75
Filmstrips, 76
Flannelboards, 76, 77
Flashcards, 76, 78
Folklore, 78-79
Follow-up, conferences, 41
Fo net ik, 52-53
Food, 79-80
Fractions, 139
Future, 80

G

Games, 81-82, 86-87
Geography:
    cities, 85
    climate, 84
    directions, 85
    earth-sun relationships, 85-86
    earth's surface, 82, 84
    games, 86-87
    natural resources, 84
    population, 84-85
    water, 84
    world regions, 85
Geometry, 134-136
Gifted child, 87
Grammar, 88-89
Gross motor skills, slow learner, 191
Grouping, 89-90
Guidance, 90-91

H

Hawaii, 92-94
History:
  Civil War, 97
  colonial, 95-97
  Columbus, 94-95
  general, 97-98
  World Wars, 97
Holidays, 98-99
Homework, 99-100
Homonyms, 100, 101
Honor roll, 100, 102
Horoscope, 102-103

I

Ideas, 104-106
Indians, 106-108
Individualization of instruction, 109
Inquiry, 109-110
Instruction, individualization, 109
Instructional aides, 20
Instructional Media Center, 120-121
Instructor, 57
Interest centers, 110-114
Interjections, 89

J

Jolly Good Show, 52
Junk, 115

K

Kindergarten, 116-117
Kits (multimedia), 117-118
Koch, Kenneth, 57

L

Land, 61-62
Language arts, 119
Language skills, slow learner, 192
Latitude, 85
Learning, 119-120
Learning contracts, 42, 43

Lesson plans, 120
Library, 120-121
Limericks, 121
Listening, 122-123
Listening centers, 123
Longitude, 85

M

Machines, 124-125
Magazines, 125-126
Magic box, 126-127
Magic circle, 127-128
Magic square, 128-129
Maps, 129-133
Mathematics:
  basics, 136-138
  fractions, 139
  geometry, 134-136
  historical activities, 133-134
  sources for activities, 140
Media Center, 120-121
Mental development, 51
Metrics, 140-142
Mnemonic devices, 142-143
Mobiles, 143-144
Money, 64
Motivation, 144-145
Multimedia kits, 117-118
Murals, 145-146
Music, 146-148

N

Natural resources, 84
Nature, 60-61
Newspapers, 149-156
Noise pollution, 63
Nonsense words, 53
Nouns, 88

O

Objectives, 157-158
Ole!, 52
Open House, 128
Open space, 158-159
Organization, 159-160

Outlining, 160-161
Overhead projector, 162

P

Parent-teacher conference, 39-41
Penmanship, 163-164
Perceptual motor skills, slow learner, 191-192
Phonograph records, 182
Photography, 164-165
Physical development, 50
Physical education, 165-166
Picture file, 55
Plants, 166-168
Plays, writing, 57
Poetry:
    colorful, 170
    diamante, 170-171
    haiku, 170
    noise, 169
    shape, 168-169
    suggestions, 171
Pollution (*see* Ecology)
Population, 84-85
Posters, 171-172
Prefixes, 180-181
Prepositions, 89
Pretending, 172
Production, 64-65
Projective techniques, 173
Projector, overhead, 162
Projects, art, 23-24, 56
Pronouns, 88
Puzzles, 173-174

Q

Questions, 175-176
Quiet center, 176-177

R

Reading:
    consonant blends, 178-179
    consonants, 178
    critical, 47
    digraphs, 179

Reading *(cont.)*.
    prefixes, 180-181
    suffixes, 181-182
    vowels, 179-180
Records (phonograph), 182
Records (school and classroom), 183
Reports, book, 27-28
Resources, natural, 84
Rewards, 183
Role playing, 183-185

S

Science, 186
Seasons:
    fall, 188-189
    spring, 188
    summer, 188
    winter, 187-188
Self-concept, 189
Sensory-motor skills, slow learner, 191
Slides, 189-190
Slow learner:
    conceptual skills, 192
    gross motor skills, 191
    language skills, 192
    perceptual motor skills, 191-192
    sensory-motor skills, 191
    social acceptance, 192-193
Social development, 50
Sound (noise pollution), 63
Space, 193-194
Spelling, 194-195
Sports, 195-197
Spring, 188
Spring Fever, 197-198
Stamps (postage), 198
Substitutes, 198-199
Suffixes, 181-182
Summer, 188
Sun, 85-86
Supplemental materials, 56
Synonyms, 199-201

T

Tape recorder, 202-203
Task cards, 203

Teacher, 57
Teacher:
    activities, 55-56
    as counselor, 90-91
Television, 203-204
Tests, achievement, 16-17
Textbooks, 204-205
Transparencies, 205
Transportation, 205-206
Trips, 74
Typewriter, 206-207

U

Units of study, 208

V

Values, 209-210
Verbs, 88
Vocabulary, 210
Volcano, 210-211
Vowels, 179-180

W

Water, 62-63, 84
Weather, 212
Winter, 187-188
Words:
    action, 17-18
    nonsense, 53
Worksheets, 56
World regions, 85
World Wars, 97
Writing, creative, 44-45

Y

Yes or No Game, 52

Z

Zip Code, U.S.A., 213-215